Praise for the plays of Mark Jackson

God's Plot

"*God's Plot is a complex yet seemingly effortless hybrid. Nods to Shakespeare and pokes at theatrical process comfortably mingle with critiques of Puritan society and allusions to today's moral conundrums. It's a largely comic evening of serious ideas... An adventuresome delight.*"
— VARIETY

"*Jackson's portrait of life in the colony is gripping... This provocative piece grapples with a tangle of issues, from the love of spectacle that dominates both theater and religion and narcissism of the artist to the price paid for heroism in a cowardly time. But perhaps the most potent theme is the long and storied history of protest in this country... The palpable sense of patriotism generated in the play's closing moments leaves a lump in your throat.*"
— SAN JOSE MERCURY NEWS

"*God's Plot is a rousing success... The dialogue mixes archaic and modern language to great comic effect... Well crafted, comprehensible, and wildly entertaining, it's a fabulous addition to Jackson's oeuvre.*"
— EAST BAY EXPRESS

Mary Stuart

"*Mark Jackson's radical adaptation is stark, direct and unornamented, and as cruel as a conspirator's smile. Jackson has stripped more than an hour, maybe a dozen characters and a lot of romanticism from Schiller's overstuffed text... The essence of the broader stakes remains, with sharper currency, in the riveting verbal duels, plots and jockeying for power.*"
— SAN FRANCISCO CHRONICLE

"A claustrophobic immorality play, a paranoid thriller... Unsettlingly atemporal... Mary Stuart is a chilling piece... It feels frighteningly intimate."
— THE DAILY CALIFORNIAN

"Mark Jackson has adapted the play into a modern political thriller, with terrorism, national security and sexual tension each playing their part as Mary struggles for her life... Jackson's fast-paced production easily builds tension with his rhythmic use of language punctuated with total silence."
— CONTRA COSTA TIMES

Salomania

"Maud Allan has long deserved a play of her own, and she gets a brilliant one in Mark Jackson's Salomania... It's an incisive courtroom drama... An intriguing biography of an exceptional woman, and an instructive look at an era not unlike our own... Riveting... Haunting... Salomania is sensational."
— SAN FRANCISCO EXAMINER

"Salomania, written and directed by Mark Jackson, is a spectacular play in all senses of the word. Reeling between the trenches of World War I and an uproarious courtroom drama as funny as it is disturbing, it spins out a staggering constellation of questions relating theater and war, art and politics, beauty and brutality... Fantastically entertaining throughout and studded with scenes of profound relevance and philosophical weight, Salomania is a brilliant play as substantial as it is well composed."
— SFAPPEAL.COM

"Wildly ambitious... Like all of Jackson's plays, Salomania brims with big ideas, almost to the point of overreaching. Somehow, it's still masterful... Jackson pulls it all together by placing high demands on everyone, including the audience... That it coheres in the end—and even resonates with contemporary politics—is a triumph."
— EAST BAY EXPRESS

Mark Jackson

THREE PLAYS

Three Plays – *God's Plot, Mary Stuart* and *Salomania*
by Mark Jackson
Copyright © 2012 by Mark Jackson
All rights reserved

Published by EXIT PRESS
First Edition: November 2012

Cover design by Kevin Clarke.
Book design by Richard Livingston.
Front cover photo by Pak Han, used with permission, from the 2011 Shotgun Players world premiere production of *God's Plot*. Visit Pak Han at www.pakhan.com

CAUTION: Professionals and amateurs are hereby warned that the plays represented in this book are subject to a royalty. All rights of every kind to these plays belong to their author, Mark Jackson. These plays are protected by United States and international copyright laws. These laws ensure the author is rewarded for his work and protected against theft or abuse of that work. To secure rights for theatrical production, or for any other public or private use of these plays, in part or in whole, go to www.artstreettheatre.org to contact the author and negotiate a legal contract with all relevant details, among them rights and payment of royalties. This is true for academic, amateur, professional, or any other producers.

In addition to not performing or otherwise publicly using these plays without obtaining prior written permission from the author and without paying the requisite royalty, please do not photocopy, scan, or by any other method duplicate any part of this book as such actions also constitute a violation of the law.

For additional information about U.S. copyright laws, go to www.copyright.gov.
For additional information about Mark Jackson, go to www.artstreettheatre.org.

Some of the plays in this collection contain stage directions suggesting the use of specific works of music. EXIT Press has not obtained permissions for the use of these works of music. Any producer of these plays electing to use these works of music in production is advised to obtain the necessary permissions, and, toward that end, to consult the above listed U.S. Copyright Office website, as well as that of ASCAP (www.ascap.com), BMI (www.bmi.com), or NMPA (www.nmpa.org) as applicable.

Paperback ISBN: 978-0-9856584-2-7

EXIT PRESS
156 Eddy Street
San Francisco, CA 94102-2708
mail@theexit.org

To Beth
for love and support.

To Kevin
for friendship and meticulousness.

To both
for having each brought their artistry
to the original productions of two of these plays,
as well as many, many others.
Thank you!

Contents

Foreword by Patrick Dooley	ix
God's Plot	1
Mary Stuart	69
Salomania	105
Notes on the Plays	173
About the Author	177

Foreword

My first encounter with Mark Jackson came in the form of an 8.5 x 11 newsletter photocopied on bright red paper. I saw it next to a pile of theater handbills while browsing through the now defunct Limelight Bookstore in San Francisco some time in the late 90's. I can't remember what subjects were touched (torched!) on, but I was immediately struck by the uncompromising passion and joy in the words. It wasn't just a call to "save the world with art." It went a step further, implying that mediocre, lazy theater weakened our civilization. That bright red manifesto felt like a thrown gauntlet to this fellow young theater maker. Go hard or go home!

It's impossible for me to write about Mark Jackson the playwright without also saying something about him as a director. He is meticulous with every detail, pursues his vision with rigor and is always the most prepared person in the room. The respect he brings to his craft fosters an intense loyalty with his collaborators. Sitting with Mark in a late-night, tech-week production meeting as we hash over the minutiae of a sound cue I am reminded of his newsletters. It's not that civilization will rise or fall based on the artistry of a single production. The point is that a society is made stronger by our decisions as individuals to do whatever we choose to do with intention, thoughtfulness and a spirit of curiosity—qualities that have served Mark equally well as a playwright. I can say without reservation that no playwright/director in the Bay Area, a region increasingly known for its new work, has achieved such a consistent degree of critical and box office success as Mark Jackson over the last ten years.

This success is not born from Mark's facility with writing the contemporary "well-made play," a 90-minute 3-to-5 hander on a unit set with some charming, slightly damaged characters struggling with the challenges of modern day America. He hasn't, to my knowledge, ever written such a thing. Theaters stretched for finances and struggling for audiences gravitate to these pieces because they're more affordable to produce and intellectually accessible to a broad audience. One leaves the performance of the "well-made play" discussing the witty dialogue, the tidy resolution of the drama and the comfort that all is well in the world. The "well-made play" does well for the same reasons that we choose McDonalds and Ivory soap and their cousin television: it's predictable.

The plays in this collection defy this conventional wisdom. They are sweeping epics with heightened language, swirling narrative structures and fantastical stage directions. Jackson has created worlds that demand every designer in the room bring their most creative spirits to the table. Sets and costumes must be as alive and nimble as the performers. And so must the audience! Because while these plays are wildly entertaining, what distinguishes them is that they have some of the most important questions of our time—what is freedom? what is terrorism? what does it mean to live in a democracy?—woven into their fabric.

Theater by its very live nature calls out to be a place for engagement, stimulation, catharsis. Let's pick up that gauntlet Jackson throws down and continue the conversation.

Patrick Dooley
Artistic Director, The Shotgun Players
August 2012

God's Plot

God's Plot

God's Plot was originally commissioned and produced by The Shotgun Players, Berkeley, CA. Patrick Dooley, Artistic Director. Liz Lisle, Managing Director. The world premiere was given there on December 3, 2011. The production was directed by the author, with the following cast and staff:

WILLIAM DARBY	Carl Holvick-Thomas
TRYAL PORE	Juliana Lustenader
DANIEL PRICHARD	Joseph Salazar
CORNELIUS WATKINS	Anthony Nemirovsky
JOHN FAWSETT	Dave Maier
PHILLIP HOWARD / HARBOR CLERK	William Hand
EDWARD MARTIN / HOWELL CROSS / BRISTOL JUDGE	John Mercer
EDMOND PORE / GEORGE DERBY	Kevin Clarke
CONSTANCE PORE / MARY TAYLOR	Fontana Butterfield
THOMAS FOWKES	Dan Bruno
MUSICIANS	Travis Kindred, Josh Pollock

Songs Composed by	Daveen Digiacomo
Underscoring created by	Travis Kindred and Josh Pollock
Scenery	Nina Ball
Costumes	Christine Crook
Lights	Heather Basarab
Properties	Jacqueline Scott
Stage Manager	Amanda Krieger

Dramatis Personae

> *Eight men and two women play the various roles. All characters are Puritan unless otherwise noted. Though the estimated ages of the historical figures are listed, casting need not adhere to this in all cases.*
>
> *William Darby – an artistic personality with a past, no religion but passes as Puritan, age 25.*
> *Tryal Pore – daughter of Captain Edmond Pore, and an independent spirit, age 17.*
> *Daniel Prichard – a carpenter, two years out of his indentured servitude,*

age 27.
Cornelius Watkins – an only recently-achieved middle class landowner now already on hard times, age 23.
John Fawsett – Sheriff of Accomack County, age 38.
Phillip Howard – a former indentured servant only recently turned tenant hand, age 20.
Edward Martin – a perpetual indentured servant and Quaker, age 49.
Captain Edmond Pore – Captain in His Majesty's service, Judge in the Accomack County Court, age 42.
Constance Pore – wife of Captain Edmond Pore, age 37.
Thomas Fowkes – a tavern keeper and Quaker, age 35.
Major Howell Cross – local representative at Jamestown of His Majesty's Council Appointed to Foreign Plantations, age 45.
Mary Taylor.
George Derby.
A Bristol Judge.
A troupe of players.
A Harbor Clerk.
Other roles in Scene One as needed.

In addition, there is a small band of musicians to provide live accompaniment for the songs, as well as underscoring for scenes as deemed appropriate.

Time and Place

Summer and Autumn, 1665, in Pungoteague, Accomack County, on the Eastern Shore of the New World's Virginia Colony.

Set

The Pore family barn. Everywhere Darby went on his journey from England to the New World. Outside Cornelius Watkins' (later Daniel Prichard's) home. The shoreline of a creek running along the Smith property. A montage of daily-life locations in Pungoteague. The kitchen and dining area inside the Pore family home. Fowkes' Tavern. A remote clearing in the woods.

Music

The music should not seek to imitate music from the 1665 American colonial period anymore than it should strive to make a point of being anachronistically contemporary. Tryal Pore's "unholy music" should be somehow beyond time, something slightly unruly that has come from her and reflects her personality. The five songs sung by Tryal Pore should be used as a starting point for creating the underscoring of scenes and transitions. Though the script does indicate certain moments to be underscored, underscoring should be used where a given production deems appropriate.

Producers who wish to use Daveen Digiacomo's music for their production of God's Plot should contact her through Mark Jackson at www.artstreettheatre.org.

Notes

A slash in the dialogue (/) indicates that the next actor should start their line, creating overlapping speech.

Texts in [brackets] are alternate possibilities according to the staging.

Act One
Scene One

In the barn on the Pore property. TRYAL PORE talks to an imaginary group of people. WILLIAM DARBY listens intently from the side.

TRYAL PORE I confess it, I was distracted from the true path, lured into the grove by an unholy siren. Listening here every Sabbath in our house of worship to the music of our Lord, sung in praise of Him by you my good friends and neighbors, I felt in my heart a great distance from God. I sought to bridge this chasm with a mistaken music, which spoke not in praise of Almighty God, but rather my own heart, my own self, my own false independence from the Lord our Father. As my neighbors sang the true holy melody, I sat amongst them and imagined the discords of my own unholy anthem. And I mistook this inner music for true freedom. Then, on Sabbath last, this inward jangling burst outward from inside me. God had ripped my inner voice out from the echo chamber of my breast and exposed it to every ear. It jolted me,

WILLIAM DARBY No:

TRYAL PORE It jolted me!

WILLIAM DARBY Better:

TRYAL PORE It JOLTED me!

WILLIAM DARBY Good!

TRYAL PORE Like lightning upon the earth! And I found myself struck amazed, as you my neighbors rightly were. Hearing myself then, finally in the heat of full voice, at once I understood the true tenor of this wicked siren that had chilled my heart with its icy breath. My open guilt schooled me at once,

WILLIAM DARBY "My Open Guilt / SCHOOLED me–"

TRYAL PORE My Open Guilt SCHOOLED me at once, and brought my true heart back to the one true music–

WILLIAM DARBY "–Back to the ONE TRUE MUSIC!"

TRYAL PORE Back to the ONE TRUE MUSIC and the SPIRIT of the Lord JESUS CHRIST ALMIGHTY! I pray He forgive me! And I sing now ONLY for HIM!

  ...TRYAL PORE looks to WILLIAM DARBY.

WILLIAM DARBY ...Good.

TRYAL PORE You can tell me.

WILLIAM DARBY It's good. "Every Sabbath" is good. It reminds them you're in regular attendance.

TRYAL PORE I am. Every Sabbath. Without fail.

WILLIAM DARBY "Lured into the grove by an unholy siren" is good.

TRYAL PORE I like that line.

WILLIAM DARBY By the end I still don't feel a strong enough sense for what's at stake.

TRYAL PORE It's my delivery.

WILLIAM DARBY Maybe I need to add some lines. Something to help it finally ERUPT.

TRYAL PORE Or I need to act it better.

WILLIAM DARBY No, what you're doing is nice. Maybe that's the problem. It's too nice.

TRYAL PORE I do feel I flatter them a bit much. "My good friends." You my neighbors were "rightly" amazed. Is it too obvious?

WILLIAM DARBY Not too. But anyway they like to be flattered.

TRYAL PORE Yes.

WILLIAM DARBY Ultimately what we need is the unequivocal sense that you are DRIVEN by your guilt. That it TEARS at your soul. That by the end you even drop to your knees and I hate to say it but I think you need to cry.

TRYAL PORE Oh!

WILLIAM DARBY I know.

TRYAL PORE I hate that! Everyone does that! It's such a cliche!

WILLIAM DARBY You don't need to ACTUALLY cry. They need to BELIEVE that you cry. They need to feel they've seen real tears. If they think they have, then for all intents and purposes they have and your work is done. I always say: The scene is ever about / the other person.

TRYAL PORE The other person, yes, but this is not a scene. It's a monologue. I'll be up there in front of the congregation by myself.

WILLIAM DARBY And so your fellow actor IS the congregation. It's them you must change, not yourself. THEY must believe. THEY must understand your guilt and your epiphany. And tears would be an outward sign of this.

TRYAL PORE If I put on a spectacle of tears they won't believe it because I don't believe it. It's not honest. You want me to feel everything but I tell you honestly I feel nothing. I'm only doing this / because–

WILLIAM DARBY You do not have to feel everything. You actually need to NOT feel everything. Half the emotion is for you, and the other half is for them. That's why they come. They just want to FEEL something – in this case your guilt, their forgiveness, and the security of their superiority. So long as you make them feel those things, they'll forgive you any number of sins. Know your audience.

TRYAL PORE I'll work on it.

WILLIAM DARBY And it will be great. It needs to be. Remember what happened to Lizzie Crackborn. You don't want this to end like it did for her.

TRYAL PORE No.

WILLIAM DARBY And, you being Tryal Pore, beautiful daughter of Edmond Pore, local Court Judge and Harbor Captain in His Majesty's Service, makes it all the more important.

TRYAL PORE I know it.

WILLIAM DARBY Okay then. ...And I'll rewrite the ending. Fire up the sturm und drang.

TRYAL PORE The what?

WILLIAM DARBY It means the drama.

TRYAL PORE You speak foreign tongues.

WILLIAM DARBY I've picked up a few here and there.

TRYAL PORE Where and where?

WILLIAM DARBY *(changing the subject)* Well, Goody Pore; we have completed your reading lesson, we have rehearsed your confession; our appointment today is done.

TRYAL PORE Now what?

WILLIAM DARBY Now we say Farewell.

TRYAL PORE Come here.

WILLIAM DARBY Tryal Pore, you will have yourself clapped in the stocks for a greater sin before you've confessed your present one. One sin at a time, my Lady.

TRYAL PORE I'll take them as they see fit to come.

WILLIAM DARBY Your heart beats to its own strange drum.

TRYAL PORE You make my heart's red blood race.

WILLIAM DARBY You'd make red an ivory face.

TRYAL PORE True! I see YOU blush whenever I sit close while you teach me.

I hear your breathing change each time both our hands reach for the same page and brush against each other.

WILLIAM DARBY You know I think fondly of you. But here in your family's barn, like animals, while your mother and father think I'm tutoring you.

TRYAL PORE You do tutor me.

WILLIAM DARBY In the ways of letters.

TRYAL PORE And the ways of the great wide world. When will you take me to your world?

WILLIAM DARBY It's the same world as yours.

TRYAL PORE You know what I'm asking. What life did you live before like magic you appeared out of nowhere on the Eastern Shores of Virginia?

WILLIAM DARBY That life's the past. It doesn't exist.

TRYAL PORE Why must you be so mysterious? I ask and ask. Now tell me. Who were you?

WILLIAM DARBY What difference does it make who I was? You know me as I am.

TRYAL PORE Were you a pirate?

WILLIAM DARBY From time to time.

TRYAL PORE A heathen?

WILLIAM DARBY Some would say.

TRYAL PORE Would they? Who? What would they say? ...William Darby. I long to know once and for all who is this man that holds my heart in his hand. If you have secrets, they are safe with me. You know it. Tell me your story.

> *WILLIAM DARBY regards TRYAL PORE with a flirty combination of fondness and suspicion for a long moment, then makes a show of relenting:*

WILLIAM DARBY ...Once upon a time in a far off land called England.

> *TRYAL PORE claps her hands giddily and positions herself as audience to WILLIAM DARBY'S story, which is at once underscored by music. Other ACTORS enter and help enact the tale as it is told.*

WILLIAM DARBY There lived in the county of Somerset an unfortunate young woman called Mary Taylor, who met a young rascal, himself called George Derby. George Derby, it is said, had two green eyes that could between them snatch from the air any dove or sparrow. Thus snatched, Mary Taylor promptly professed to George Derby her undying love. They had not yet wed by the time Mary Taylor found she'd conceived, at which time George Derby found cause to take the low road that ran out of town and on to the sea... Their bastard was born in an old crow's cabin, and not without effort from Mary. When the ordeal was done, and the child in her arms, with her last breath she named it:

MARY TAYLOR   George Junior.

WILLIAM DARBY   Then she fainted and fell into Lucifer's lap, where to this day the Somerset locals refer any traveler who comes seeking the final resting place of that unfortunate young woman, Mary Taylor... Well, the old crow raised the bastard until he reached boyhood, then sold him to a traveling troupe. This troupe trouped in secret for fear of that noose that Cromwell had hung to catch players. Thus young George grew up amongst actors and thieves, learning both trades by apprentice. And learned he did. By the time George reached the age of nineteen, he could woo and roar on command, swashbuckle on stage and off, enunciate his way through any advantageous opening, and orate himself out of any tightcorner... Then, one dark day, treachery struck the troupe. One of the players succumbed first to hunger, thence to a bribe, and tattled to Cromwell's well-fed cronies, who ambushed the troupe in one fell swoop when in Bristol they'd set their stage in a Lord's private parlor. Now dragged into court and faced with a judge, George found himself suddenly on his own. His family of players, to his great surprise, all played their own hands, each seeking mercy unto themselves. So much for a troupe and that all-for-one spirit they'd touted. So when the judge declared:

BRISTOL JUDGE   "Hie ye to four years in prison, you actors!"

WILLIAM DARBY   George saw at once both his corner and opening. He knelt with a show of most eloquent reverence, and brokered a deal all his own. Rather than prison, he'd take a new life, and to the old Judge he proposed: "Indenture me six years to serve in Barbados any entrepreneur who needs bodies. I'll cut down the jungle, shovel earth into swamps, lay stones for his great wealth's foundation."

BRISTOL JUDGE   "Sold!"

WILLIAM DARBY   Said the Judge. And so it was that the very next day at Bristol's docks, the bastard George Derby Junior boarded a ship bound and determined for a new world of adventure in the Colony Barbados! ... For the next weeks the ship rose and fell on wave after wave. Whether up or down, George kept his eye steadfastly on the horizon, painting on that distant canvas a map of the treasures awaiting him there... One day, another man came and stood next to George. His name was Daniel.

DANIEL PRICHARD   "Daniel Prichard."

WILLIAM DARBY   "Glad to meet you, Daniel Prichard."

DANIEL PRICHARD   "And you, sir?"

WILLIAM DARBY   "I am the bastard George Derby Junior."

DANIEL PRICHARD   "I've noticed you share my fondness for the horizon, George Derby Junior. What hopes have YOU hung there?"

WILLIAM DARBY   "A new adventure awaits me across that line. I hear that in the Colony Barbados exotic possibilities bend down the jungle's branches like thick clusters of ripe fruits, so easy for picking."

DANIEL PRICHARD "Those jungles are thick with ripe fruits indeed – to HARVEST, not to own. And swamps that, once drained, are flooded with sweat from lifting bone-crushing stones to lay the foundation of some gentleman's wealth. Beneath that foundation lie buried the men who dropped the stones to swat the mosquitoes, fattened with blood and plague. I wouldn't go to Barbados for love or for money. It's the devil's Colony."

WILLIAM DARBY "What Colony are YOU bound to then, if not Barbados?"

DANIEL PRICHARD "One far less exotic, but infinitely more practical. Virginia."

WILLIAM DARBY "Virginia. What possible adventure awaits you in Virginia?"

DANIEL PRICHARD "A new life in God's New World."

WILLIAM DARBY "GOD'S New World. Not England's?"

DANIEL PRICHARD "No world belongs to any man or country. God has opened this New World to reward those with patience and forethought."

WILLIAM DARBY "Afore what, may I ask, are you thinking so patiently?"

DANIEL PRICHARD "My future. Four years of indentured servitude buy my passage to this New World, and, upon arrival, a solid foothold on the well-established tobacco plantation of one Richard Ditty, a gentleman in Bristol who's never seen his venture with his own eyes. His hands built nothing, but they sewed the purse. My hands know carpentry. After four years of sawing Ditty's wood and hammering his nails, I'll be a free man and poised to establish my own plot, make of my own wood and nails a house, a barn and a carpentry shed. Upon the shed I'll hang a sign, on it writ 'open for business.' In the barn I'll house my animals for the winter. In the house, a wife by summer. And the following spring, our children."

WILLIAM DARBY "Practical."

DANIEL PRICHARD "Paradise, Mister Derby. Paradise."

WILLIAM DARBY regards the horizon.

WILLIAM DARBY The carpenter, Daniel Prichard, had painted over the bastard George Derby Junior's exotic canvas with a wash of practical blue. Suddenly George saw the sky as it was – a beautiful, simple hue. For what did the red Barbados skies promise? Six years hacking at jungles? Filling swamps with his sweat and blood? Breaking his bones for some other man's foundation? Prichard's paradise suddenly seemed infinitely more practical indeed... So, when the Barbados-bound ship took its rest stop at Virginia, rather than bid the carpenter farewell, George helped him row his boat to shore, whereon, mustering his former actorly skills, he passed himself off as "a free man of moderate means, having spent said means on avoyage across the sea." And when the Harbor Clerk asked for his paternal name:

HARBOR CLERK "Paternal Name?"

With a wink and a shush to DANIEL PRICHARD, who is next in line, WILLIAM DARBY answers:

WILLIAM DARBY "Darby," said Derby. And for a given name he plagiarized that of his favorite playwright:

HARBOR CLERK "Given Name?"

WILLIAM DARBY William.

HARBOR CLERK "William Darby, welcome to Virginia. Next!"

WILLIAM DARBY bids DANIEL PRICHARD goodbye and moves on.

WILLIAM DARBY And so William Darby set to work. A literate fellow with a gift for the pen, he made ends meet with this job and that – here a clerk, there a merchant's record keeper, now scribe to a small business owner, now tutor to children of well-to-do gooders. William's talent for letters proved rare in these parts, and hence of great use to the farmer-bound town. And thus it was that William Darby found himself both established and free – not in exotic Barbados, but the burgeoning town called Pungoteague, Accomack County, neatly nestled on the Eastern Shore of England's – or God's – Colony Virginia. A new home, for a new life, in a New World.

WILLIAM DARBY'S story has come to an end.

TRYAL PORE ...The end?

WILLIAM DARBY The beginning.

TRYAL PORE But what of the dramatic scene in which the adventuresome William Darby meets Tryal Pore, beautiful daughter of Edmond Pore, local Court Judge and Harbor Captain in His Majesty's Service, and William falls dangerously in love with her, and: vows to fulfill her every last wish?

WILLIAM DARBY Is that how his story ends?

TRYAL PORE Begins!

WILLIAM DARBY Tryal Pore, beautiful daughter of Edmond Pore, local Court Judge and Harbor Captain in His Majesty's Service, of whom William is dangerously fond, what is your every last wish?

TRYAL PORE To make love with you.

WILLIAM DARBY Tryal. You know it would be fornication.

TRYAL PORE It would not be fornication. It would be love.

WILLIAM DARBY ...Being a freelance free spirit, I consent.

TRYAL PORE leaps at WILLIAM DARBY.

WILLIAM DARBY But not now!

TRYAL PORE Ah! When then?

WILLIAM DARBY When we know we'll not be discovered.

TRYAL PORE You are as practical as Daniel Prichard. Must I wait four years, an indentured servant to your new found practicality? Are you ashamed of me?

WILLIAM DARBY Not ashamed.

TRYAL PORE Afraid, then?

WILLIAM DARBY Of you?

TRYAL PORE Of my siren's unholy music.

WILLIAM DARBY Let's wait until the siren has successfully confessed her sin.

TRYAL PORE You don't believe in these confessions any more than I do.

WILLIAM DARBY It doesn't matter what we believe, but what our friends and neighbors do.

TRYAL PORE You don't believe THAT either.

WILLIAM DARBY No. But they do. And there are more of them than of us.

TRYAL PORE William Darby!

WILLIAM DARBY Tryal Pore. It's practical.

And WILLIAM DARBY dashes away. TRYAL PORE is alone. TRYAL PORE sings her unholy music:

TRYAL PORE *(sings)*
Once upon
It was a matter of time
The New World
Already fashioned so old
Old world olden scold world
Old says no to bold world

Take a voyage across the sea
To an island called independence me
Born without a sail to hoist
Born a kid without much choice
Born to be and born too wild
Born to get ready, don't bore this child

Once upon
It was a matter of time
The New World
Already fashioned so old

Old world olden scold world
Old says no to bold world

To my skin if only he
Learn my body by taking me
Tear from off my proper dress
Tear the moon down make a mess
Tear the rule and tear the book
Tear thou shalt not with a look

Dig down in my breast to find
Play the anthem I call mine
Sing to Heaven, lean to Hell
Sing the hero and ne'erdowell
Sing for honest, sing the call
Sing the song that speaks for us all

Once upon
It was a matter of time
The New World
Already fashioned so old
Old world olden scold world
Old says no to bold world
Old world olden scold world
Old world now the bold world

Scene Two

> *Outside the home of CORNELIUS WATKINS. JOHN FAWSETT is knocking on the front door.*

JOHN FAWSETT Cornelius Watkins! It's John Fawsett... Cornelius, are you to home?

> *CORNELIUS WATKINS enters from elsewhere.*

JOHN FAWSETT Cornelius Wat–! There you are. I thought you might be hiding.

CORNELIUS WATKINS What can I do for you, Sheriff Fawsett?

JOHN FAWSETT No need to be so formal, Cornelius, I haven't any warrant for you.

CORNELIUS WATKINS What brings you out here then, Sheriff Fawsett?

JOHN FAWSETT You are intent on suspicion. SHOULD I have a warrant for you?

CORNELIUS WATKINS No. You'll pardon me, John. This tobacco season has left me wary. May I offer you a chair? You'll find it inside next to the table with the plate and the crumbs. Oh, and there's an empty pan on the hearth. Everything else I sold to keep that much.

JOHN FAWSETT Sorry to hear it's come to that. What are you sleeping on these days, then, the table or the plate?

CORNELIUS WATKINS The straw.

JOHN FAWSETT You're not sleeping in your barn?

CORNELIUS WATKINS What's left of the livestock sleep in what's left of the barn. I brought what's left of a bail of straw inside for what's left of a good night's rest.

JOHN FAWSETT Well, this tobacco season has been rough on a good many people.

CORNELIUS WATKINS That doesn't ease my suffering.

JOHN FAWSETT Maybe it helps to know you're not alone.

CORNELIUS WATKINS That is the trouble. Too many tobacco farmers with too many bumper crops. The tobacco market is flooded. Prices sunk to the bottom of the ocean. And his Majesty's new Trade Law is the anchor. You tell me: what sense does it make that I should sell exclusively to London merchants, while they sell to all of Europe? Makes sense to THEM, who have His Majesty's ear. It's hard to be heard from across the Atlantic. Forty thousand souls on this Eastern Shore have been impoverished to enrich forty London merchants, who now have forty thousand SERVANTS thus at cheap rates. I paid my dues of indentured servitude already. Here I am now a servant once again.

JOHN FAWSETT You are as free as the crows, and make your own choices just as freely. Did His Majesty force you to buy four hundred fifty acres you couldn't afford? Did the London merchants force you to put up your first crop as credit? You signed your name to that loan; no one held the pen for you.

CORNELIUS WATKINS I was told it was a standard arrangement.

JOHN FAWSETT And I happen to know, Cornelius, that you signed a false claim to having nine heads on hand. A man can't get a patent for four hundred fifty acres without nine indentured servants set to work it. That's the law.

CORNELIUS WATKINS I had workers.

JOHN FAWSETT Itinerant labor up from the Spanish colonies, despite plenty of good Englishmen right here in Accomack County, hungry and able.

CORNELIUS WATKINS It's a lie. Who told you I hired Spanish colony labor?

JOHN FAWSETT No one told me. I have eyes. Ears, too. And didn't I look the other way and whistle?

CORNELIUS WATKINS I thank you for that. Anyway I'm not the only man to adjust his numbers and hire on the sly.

JOHN FAWSETT You're not the only one paying for it now either. I said I didn't come with a warrant for you. But I did come with some advice. There are people you owe money asking me to lean on you. Some have been talking to Judge Pore directly.

CORNELIUS WATKINS Judge Pore doesn't have time to worry about one more indebted tobacco farmer.

JOHN FAWSETT All the same, best to add your numbers properly and hire locally from now on, Cornelius. You've had enough trouble, don't you think?

CORNELIUS WATKINS I thank you for the advice, John. I'll be out of trouble soon.

JOHN FAWSETT That sounds like confidence. Where'd you get it?

CORNELIUS WATKINS A carpenter built it for me.

JOHN FAWSETT A carpenter? I know you don't mean Jesus, Cornelius Watkins. Best not to make riddles with God.

CORNELIUS WATKINS God's made plenty of those Himself. I mean a carpenter, name of Daniel Prichard, I'm hoping wants to buy my land, set up a homestead and carpentry business for himself. Make his future, he says.

JOHN FAWSETT That would go some ways to ease your suffering.

CORNELIUS WATKINS This land was supposed to be MY future!

DANIEL PRICHARD arrives.

DANIEL PRICHARD Good day, Mister Watkins!

CORNELIUS WATKINS Speak of the devil.

DANIEL PRICHARD Your pardon?

CORNELIUS WATKINS Daniel Prichard. This is John Fawsett, Accomack County Sheriff, if you haven't had cause to know him already.

DANIEL PRICHARD We haven't yet had such cause. But I know of him. I hear you're a fair man Sheriff Fawsett.

JOHN FAWSETT I try to be so. I understand you're in the carpentry business, Mister Prichard.

DANIEL PRICHARD I am. If you need wood work done, I'll do fine work for you.

JOHN FAWSETT I'll keep that to mind. I understand you intend some business with Mister Watkins?

DANIEL PRICHARD I do.

JOHN FAWSETT Good. Then I'll leave you to it. Glad to have met you, Mister Prichard.

DANIEL PRICHARD God keep you, sir.

JOHN FAWSETT Mister Watkins.

CORNELIUS WATKINS Sheriff Fawsett.

JOHN FAWSETT exits.

CORNELIUS WATKINS So. Mister Prichard. Are you decided?

DANIEL PRICHARD Mister Watkins, I am.

CORNELIUS WATKINS prepares for the worst:

CORNELIUS WATKINS And?

DANIEL PRICHARD And I have come to shake your hand.

CORNELIUS WATKINS Well– ...Well! I am glad to hear that! A number of people will be.

DANIEL PRICHARD Our arrangement stands?

CORNELIUS WATKINS Four hundred acres belong to you; you build a cabin for me on the fifty remaining; I stay on as your tenant and hand. That brings the price per acre down for you, and keeps a roof up over my head at least.

DANIEL PRICHARD A fair bargain, I think.

CORNELIUS WATKINS Fair enough, times being what they are. Anyway, you're a reputable carpenter, so I trust the roof won't leak.

DANIEL PRICHARD Oh I'll build you a solid roof, Mister Watkins. Thanks be to God, this day has come at last. I've worked for it a long time.

CORNELIUS WATKINS So have I. No thanks to God. No offense to him neither.

DANIEL PRICHARD We find our own luck by God's light, Mister Watkins. It always shines for those who choose to look for it.

CORNELIUS WATKINS I must have been looking when a cloud was passing.

DANIEL PRICHARD Well. God saw fit to put our hands together.

CORNELIUS WATKINS At my expense, Mister Prichard.

DANIEL PRICHARD Your expense is mine now.

CORNELIUS WATKINS Alongside everything else I worked for.

DANIEL PRICHARD ...If you have regrets about our arrangement, Mister Watkins.

CORNELIUS WATKINS No. I'm glad for it. You'll pardon me, Mister Prichard. It wasn't a year ago I was standing on the brink of importance in this county. Then Fortune conspired against me. Not to mention King Charles.

DANIEL PRICHARD God has a plan for us all, Mister Watkins.

CORNELIUS WATKINS Yes. And King Charles signed it.

DANIEL PRICHARD offers his hand. CORNELIUS WATKINS shakes it and then gestures for PRICHARD to enter his new home. THEY do and CORNELIUS WATKINS shuts the door behind them.

Scene Three

A creek. EDWARD MARTIN is standing along the shore. PHILLIP HOWARD approaches on a small wooden skiff, driving it with a pole.

EDWARD MARTIN Howard! What are you paddling back this way for? I thought you were done with this stretch of creek.

PHILLIP HOWARD I have moved on from it, as you know. I've only come back for my pickaxe.

EDWARD MARTIN Don't you mean MY pickaxe?

PHILLIP HOWARD I mean MY pickaxe, Edward Martin.

EDWARD MARTIN You absconded with my hammers and spades, Phillip Howard.

PHILLIP HOWARD Those are my hammers and my spades, always have been, always will be. Now move aside and let me land.

EDWARD MARTIN You have no right to step on Mister Smith's property. You're no longer indentured to him.

PHILLIP HOWARD God denounces envy, Edward Martin.

EDWARD MARTIN I don't envy a moment of you.

PHILLIP HOWARD Oh no? Every indentured servant Mister Smith ever had has moved on except you. How long has it been? Fifteen years? Fifteen years a servant on another man's plot. Might as well have stayed in England. If you weren't such a stick in the mud you might have made a free soul of yourself years ago.

EDWARD MARTIN Don't fret over my soul. My soul is at peace. My soul harbors no thief, Phillip Coward.

PHILLIP HOWARD Quit that, and move yourself.

EDWARD MARTIN I'm standing right here. Turn yourself around and paddle back to your new master.

PHILLIP HOWARD *(proudly)* I have no master. I am set to be a tenant hand on the new land of one Daniel Prichard.

EDWARD MARTIN Tenant hand! The difference between tenant hand and indentured servant is a matter of spelling. Not that you would know it.

PHILLIP HOWARD Tenant hand is one step up. And a step's a step. I am on my way to manifesting my own destiny. I will have my own indentured servants before long, my own land, and my own free will. And you're just "standing right there" because you can't stand it, can you?

PHILLIP HOWARD has used his pole to poke at EDWARD MARTIN for emphasis. EDWARD MARTIN grabs the poking end of the pole.

EDWARD MARTIN Stand this, Phillip Coward!

EDWARD MARTIN gives the pole a yank.

PHILLIP HOWARD You instigate a physical encounter with me and I'll remind you of your age, old man. Give that pole back.

EDWARD MARTIN Give me my hammers and spades!

PHILLIP HOWARD They are not your hammers and spades!

A ridiculous struggle ensues, over the course of which EDWARD MARTIN and PHILLIP HOWARD go down, back up, switch places on land and sea, and end up right where they started, only with PHILLIP HOWARD once again in possession of his pole and EDWARD MARTIN knocked to the ground.

EDWARD MARTIN The devil take you, thief! You have stolen my possessions, and now my dignity too!

PHILLIP HOWARD If you lost you're dignity it's because you dropped it. Gather it up, I don't want it.

EDWARD MARTIN I want my hammers and spades.

PHILLIP HOWARD Then you had better buy some to call your own.

EDWARD MARTIN YOU had better go to God and beg forgiveness, Phillip Coward.

PHILLIP HOWARD Stop calling me that.

EDWARD MARTIN Thief.

PHILLIP HOWARD Shut it. I'll see you again shortly, Edward Martin, and I'll have Sheriff Fawsett at my side when I do. Then we'll see how brave your envy makes you.

EDWARD MARTIN I'm not afraid of you. I fear only God, and trust Him to do what is right by an honest man's integrity.

PHILLIP HOWARD Yes, I know the God you fear. Your God quakes inside you. And Mister Smith, too, I think. Is that why you've stayed indentured to him?

Music. Silence from EDWARD MARTIN.

PHILLIP HOWARD ...Well. That shut it. I don't suppose I'll be seeing you at MY Church this Sabbath. Judge Pore's daughter has a confession on. Should be a good one. Wouldn't want to miss it. ...Good day, Edward Martin. Back to your chores. And God save you from your ways.

PHILLIP HOWARD pushes himself away on his skiff and exits, leaving EDWARD MARTIN to seethe alone on the shore.

After a moment of seething, EDWARD MARTIN looks up to God. HE

>*closes his eyes and prays in silence, his hands open.*
>
>*TRYAL PORE enters, regarding EDWARD MARTIN at a distance.*
>
>*Finally, EDWARD MARTIN closes his hands, then opens his eyes again. HE looks after PHILLIP HOWARD, sighs away a seethe, then exits.*

Scene Four

>*TRYAL PORE sings her unholy music. Her NEIGHBORS go about their weekly chores.*

TRYAL PORE *(sings)*
Basic Monday Pungoteague,
On the Eastern Shore of Virginia,
The next five days pass much the same
With chores and frays and desire.
On Tuesday morn go feed the hens,
Fetch water from the spring.
Wednesday afternoon spin wool
And button the field with seeds.
Thursday scare the crows away
Lest Autumn barren be.
Friday when the sun grows tired
Drive the herds in droves and gaggles.
Saturday night by firelight
Sew up a week of holes.
Thus the new world narrative
Crawls east to west oh so slowly.

I have an eye on this town
Got my ear to the ground
This is a new song
It's not finished yet
The ending is only temporary
How its course will run
I'm not taking bets

>*As TRYAL PORE continues, EDWARD MARTIN and PHILLIP HOWARD get into a conflict.*

TRYAL PORE *(sings)*
Basically in Pungoteague
We work all week for the Sabbath.
The next six days, you may recall,

Have chores and frays and desire.
Between our daily work routines
We still find time for frays.
That's "frays" spelled F-R-A-Y-S,
Not phrases in God's Good Book.
Frays or squabbles, scraps or rows,
Grab the word you like.
In the end it's just a fight
Over laws or land or hammers.
Fighting for pride, for borders
Over plans or over coins,
Why sail over oceans if
Not for a new way of thinking?

I have an eye on this town
Got my ear to the ground
This is a new song
It's not finished yet
The ending is only temporary
How its course will run
I'm not taking bets

> As TRYAL PORE continues, EDMOND PORE and CONSTANCE PORE have a secret exchange of desires.

TRYAL PORE (sings)
Thus you see in Pungoteague
We fight all week for the Sabbath.
The next six days as you might guess
More chores and frays and desire.
"But what of that desire?" you ask.
"Tryal Pore, you have not said."
Nor has anybody else
And silence says it all.
Any woman, any man,
Alone or in the church,
Feel their skin beneath their clothes
And their hearts beneath their breastbones.
Fingers entwined in prayer to God
Convince the mind of order.
In our bones we long to touch
Young freedom's sweet lover, Chaos.

I have an eye on this town
Got my ear to the ground
This is a new song

It's not finished yet
The ending is only temporary
How its course will run
I'm not taking bets

>   As TRYAL PORE continues, her NEIGHBORS congregate in the Church.

TRYAL PORE (sings)
Finally in Pungoteague
We come to a special Sabbath.
The last six days as you have seen
had chores and frays and desire.
The congregation gathers now
To witness Tryal Pore,
Who must confess unholy thoughts
To satisfy one and all.
Every word, every move
rehearsed within an inch.
Turn this phrase. Now lift your hands.
Tear your heart and pull your guts out.
Fingers entwined in prayer to God
Convince the mob of order.
This is how we make amends
Between our minds and bodies.

TRYAL PORE (speaks) Take me back! Take me back to the ONE TRUE MUSIC and the SPIRIT of the Lord JESUS CHRIST ALMIGHTY! I pray He forgive me! And I sing now ONLY for HIM!

>   TRYAL PORE erupts into a show of convulsions and tears. Her NEIGHBORS all emote, praise God and lay hands upon her, then go their ways, chattering excitedly. Left alone and exhausted, TRYAL PORE brings her unholy ditty to a close.

TRYAL PORE (sings)
I have an eye on this town
Got my ear to the ground
This is a new song
It's not finished yet
The ending is only temporary
How its course will run
I'm not taking bets

Scene Five

>   At the table of the Pore home. EDMOND PORE and his wife,

CONSTANCE PORE, *are in good spirits over the success of their daughter TRYAL PORE'S confession.*

EDMOND PORE Good, my daughter. A fine confession today. Was it not a fine confession, Constance?

CONSTANCE PORE Indeed it was, Edmond. A very fine confession.

EDMOND PORE Do you doubt the congregation would agree?

CONSTANCE PORE I do not doubt it.

EDMOND PORE Nor I. A very fine confession indeed.

CONSTANCE PORE Tryal, off the floor [table], supper is ready.

TRYAL PORE gets up off the floor [or climbs off the table] and takes her seat.

CONSTANCE PORE You must have a hearty appetite after today. And I've made your favorite berry pie.

TRYAL PORE Is that my reward?

CONSTANCE PORE It is our reward.

EDMOND PORE Our true reward is God's pardon, which you have earned us well.

TRYAL PORE And our neighbors' pardon?

EDMOND PORE Our neighbors are but God's lambs, as we are. The entire flock is enriched by the show of forgiveness granted today.

TRYAL PORE Granted to me.

CONSTANCE PORE Granted to us.

TRYAL PORE What sin did you commit that I confessed?

EDMOND PORE Your mother bore a daughter tainted with unholy music. And I partook in raising her.

TRYAL PORE These are your sins.

EDMOND PORE God forgive us, they are. Tryal Pore, all has been set right. Eat your supper and your heart be glad.

TRYAL PORE *(relents)* You will pardon me, father, I AM weary from my performance today. That it is done and favorably received, my heart is truly glad.

CONSTANCE PORE Amen. And a good heart it is.

EDMOND PORE Very good.

Eating.

TRYAL PORE ...Still.

EDMOND PORE clanks his fork down on his plate and musters

patience.

CONSTANCE PORE Yes, be still Tryal. You must be weary indeed, how your mind meanders. You prepared so diligently all week. Mister Darby did fine work tutoring you, did he not, Edmond.

EDMOND PORE Mister Darby earned his wages very well.

CONSTANCE PORE And left our Tryal exhausted.

TRYAL PORE I often bid Mister Darby leave me exhausted, but he will not. And so I am left with no choice but to exhaust myself.

CONSTANCE PORE Well. One gains most by one's own efforts... Eat now, Tryal. But save room for berry pie. Though I've never known our Tryal to not have room enough for berry pie. She has a boy's appetite. Sometimes I have wondered did God grant me a boy in girl's clothing, such a rascal child you were. You will make an upstanding woman yet, God be willing.

TRYAL PORE Is that the question?

CONSTANCE PORE Is what the question?

TRYAL PORE If GOD is willing to make me an upstanding woman.

EDMOND PORE Yes God is.

CONSTANCE PORE The question is, Tryal, are you willing to accept His guidance.

EDMOND PORE This is not a question. She is willing. She confessed as much before our friends and neighbors this very afternoon.

TRYAL PORE Father! This afternoon was a farce!

CONSTANCE PORE Tryal Pore!

EDMOND PORE Must you tear open at once the hole you have only just mended? Ever since that day you burst out in the Church with that unholy noise this family, my Name, has been the object of suspicion in Pungoteague and we cannot afford it!

TRYAL PORE YOU cannot.

CONSTANCE PORE "We," Tryal, you heard your Father's word. Obey it.

TRYAL PORE My Father gives his word to Jamestown. It's the powers that be in Jamestown, not in Heaven, that he fears. That his name be promoted to the Court in Jamestown is his real concern, confess to THAT.

EDMOND PORE I will not have your disrespect!

TRYAL PORE Nor I yours!

CONSTANCE PORE Tryal Pore, you do not contradict your father!

TRYAL PORE It was the truth that burst out of me that day when I finally sang aloud what I feel; and for one moment I felt what freedom must be like.

CONSTANCE PORE Dear God forgive us!

EDMOND PORE You will not say another word, Tryal Pore! I will not have it. As all God's children must respect their heavenly Father so all children are bound to respect their earthly fathers. It is the order of Heaven on earth. If you disrupt this order, my good child, it is the Devil's mischief. Am I to understand you make knowing mischief with the Devil?

TRYAL PORE If I thought the Devil would not hold me responsible for his own fears I'd gladly take his hand.

CONSTANCE PORE Oh!

CONSTANCE PORE faints.

EDMOND PORE You see what your profanities have wrought! You have slain your mother!

TRYAL PORE Oh get up Mother and don't bruise yourself, the congregation isn't here to witness your efforts.

CONSTANCE PORE Why do you torture us, child! Why do you wish Hell upon us? We have ever doted on you. Decent clothes.

EDMOND PORE Clothes.

CONSTANCE PORE A tutor.

EDMOND PORE Tutor.

CONSTANCE PORE Servants enough that you have time to read by daylight.

EDMOND PORE Daylight!

CONSTANCE PORE How many daughters can say as much?

TRYAL PORE I'd give it all away and work my fingers to the bone in rags if it meant I could speak my mind freely.

EDMOND PORE I can see no evidence whatsoever that you have ANY obstacle to speaking your mind. Your free speaking has been a curse on me since the day some dark spirit bid you babble.

TRYAL PORE I speak my heart's truth. And I wish to live it.

CONSTANCE PORE If you will live at random, Tryal, according to your heart's desire we may be sure you are no believer. Remember what happened to Lizzie Crackborn!

TRYAL PORE Mother! May one have only orderly faith in God? Explain to me then the forest with its anarchic sprouting, the sea with its crashing waves, the wind that first blows this way then all at once blasts to the contrary. God's earth is in complete disarray and we call it beautiful! Why must our souls be denied God's own unwieldy beauty?

EDMOND PORE God's holy order is laid out before us that we may strive to understand it, knowing we cannot. Our childish ignorance is no justification to throw life into further chaos.

TRYAL PORE Life is chaos, father, by God's order!

CONSTANCE PORE The Devil has her tongue, Edmond! I am sure of it! This is not our daughter speaking!

EDMOND PORE You will go to Church tomorrow morning or I will drag you there myself. You will clang the bell with your own two hands, call forth the congregation and confess these blasphemies you heave upon us!

TRYAL PORE That's a bad idea.

EDMOND PORE ..."A bad idea?" A bad idea! To save your soul! To save our family name!

TRYAL PORE I just made confession today. The congregation went home satisfied. If I confess again so soon they will only doubt your Name. Besides, if you are truly worried about your public Name then let our business be private. Say nothing of what I've said and they will know nothing.

CONSTANCE PORE Our neighbors may not see what lies in our hearts, but God surely does.

TRYAL PORE Let him. Our neighbors, I think, are less forgiving. The season has everyone on edge. They're hanging women as witches in Massachusetts for so much as saying boo to a scarecrow.

EDMOND PORE Well, they have always been rather extreme in Massachusetts.

TRYAL PORE Back anyone in Pungoteague into a corner and they'll get plenty extreme. We are only conveniently progressive here.

EDMOND PORE ...I see no way forward from this but confession.

TRYAL PORE If you feel such need then confess yourself.

EDMOND PORE Me confess? To what?

TRYAL PORE You drink in the court. Confess to that.

EDMOND PORE The court is held in Fowkes' Tavern, and yes, with a meal there, I have a drink. It is no sin.

TRYAL PORE What about aiding and abetting Thomas Fowkes?

EDMOND PORE Aiding and abetting what about Thomas Fowkes?

TRYAL PORE Thomas Fowkes is Quaker! Fowkes' Tavern is a Quaker sanctuary! Everybody whispers it! But nobody, not even the Harbor Captain and Judge, Edmond Pore, will condemn him, why?, because Thomas Fowkes pours their beer!

EDMOND PORE This is nonsense!

CONSTANCE PORE She's raving. What shall we do, Edmond? What are we to do?

TRYAL PORE You know I am right.

EDMOND PORE ...You are too rough with us, child.

TRYAL PORE I am too honest with you both.

EDMOND PORE I fear your independence of mind is the way to damnation. One must not stray.

TRYAL PORE You and mother strayed from England across the sea to this Eastern Shore. Why did you do it? For damnation? I am your journey's child. Believe it.

> ...EDMOND PORE puts a hand on TRYAL PORE'S shoulder or head uncertainly, then exits.

TRYAL PORE I'll call in Sarah and clean up.

CONSTANCE PORE Don't forget the berry pie.

> CONSTANCE PORE exits after her husband.

Scene Six

> Fowkes' Tavern. THOMAS FOWKES is tending to business. At a table sit WILLIAM DARBY, CORNELIUS WATKINS and PHILLIP HOWARD with beer.

CORNELIUS WATKINS But the Dutch are worse.

WILLIAM DARBY Worse than the Spanish?

CORNELIUS WATKINS The Dutch are as nasty as the fleas they unleashed on England. Now they want to bring their fleas here. Do you know how many of His Majesty's ships are waiting in the harbor for them?

PHILLIP HOWARD How many?

CORNELIUS WATKINS Eighteen!

PHILLIP HOWARD That's a lot.

CORNELIUS WATKINS It's a legitimate threat, those Dutch fleas.

WILLIAM DARBY Not to mention those Dutch tobacco traders.

CORNELIUS WATKINS They are to be tolerated. His Majesty's fleet should let them through.

WILLIAM DARBY And how do you manage to separate the traders from the fleas?

CORNELIUS WATKINS Dunk them in a barrel of Thomas Fowkes' beer!

> Laughter.

THOMAS FOWKES Another pint, Mister Watkins? Keeps the Dutch away.

CORNELIUS WATKINS Just their fleas, thank you. I could use their trade.

WILLIAM DARBY Aren't you DONE with this tobacco business? Daniel Prichard bought your acres, did he not?

CORNELIUS WATKINS Aak!

PHILLIP HOWARD Yeah! We're carpenters now! England has nothing over us. Shipfuls of new souls arriving on the Eastern Shore every month. Housing market just goes up! No end insight! Our future is nailed down.

CORNELIUS WATKINS And what are all those new souls going to pay for these houses with? This is still a farming county. Until those Trade Laws open up the Eastern Shore is sunk. It's criminal. Something should be done.

PHILLIP HOWARD All I know is a week ago I was an indentured servant on one of the smallest plots in the county. Today I am a tenant hand. I'm stepping up.

CORNELIUS WATKINS A week ago I was a tobacco farmer on one of the largest plots in the county. And today I am a tenant hand. And I'll be damned if I'm stepping down!

PHILLIP HOWARD Curmudgeon. You're as bad as old Edward Martin. Speaking of which, the other day I went back up creek to retrieve my remaining pickaxe from Mister Smith's property, and there was Edward Martin, guarding the shore like His Majesty's fleet. Wouldn't let me land my skiff.

CORNELIUS WATKINS Why? You got fleas?

PHILLIP HOWARD No.

WILLIAM DARBY *(suspicious like a parent)* What did you do?

PHILLIP HOWARD Edward Martin started it. He called me thief! Said I stole his hammers and spades! Huh! But I called him Quaker and that shut him right up.

CORNELIUS WATKINS Is he Quaker?

PHILLIP HOWARD I suspect it. Mister Smith too. Although I never really minded Mister Smith. He always treated me respectfully. But that Edward Martin riles me.

CORNELIUS WATKINS How does Edward Martin justify his eternal rancor? I thought Quakers preached pacifism.

WILLIAM DARBY That's assuming he IS Quaker.

CORNELIUS WATKINS Phillip Howard says he is.

PHILLIP HOWARD I only say I suspect. Mister Smith too.

WILLIAM DARBY What's your evidence?

PHILLIP HOWARD Little things: Neither of them tip their hat when they greet you. Never seem to haggle at market. And they never come to OUR Church.

WILLIAM DARBY They could be Catholic.

CORNELIUS WATKINS Edward Martin is no Catholic.

WILLIAM DARBY Why not?

CORNELIUS WATKINS For one, Catholics haggle at market. Also, the Catholics are merit mongers who think good deeds alone merit salvation. I have seen no evidence of any good deed or salvageable merit attributable to Edward Martin.

WILLIAM DARBY And what can we do to cure YOUR rancor, Cornelius Watkins?

CORNELIUS WATKINS I expect you'd know. Nothing gets you down. How's the alphabet trade?

WILLIAM DARBY In good times and bad, people need things in writing.

CORNELIUS WATKINS Maybe I should take up scribbling. ...Damn Trade Laws!

PHILLIP HOWARD Don't start.

CORNELIUS WATKINS Something should be done!

WILLIAM DARBY Then do something.

CORNELIUS WATKINS I've tried everything.

WILLIAM DARBY Have you staged a protest?

PHILLIP HOWARD Have you not been listening?

WILLIAM DARBY I mean something effective.

CORNELIUS WATKINS Like what for instance?

WILLIAM DARBY You could put on a play.

CORNELIUS WATKINS ...A play?

WILLIAM DARBY A satire. Of King Charles The Second.

PHILLIP HOWARD A play?

CORNELIUS WATKINS It's blasphemy.

WILLIAM DARBY That depends.

CORNELIUS WATKINS Anyway, how would I put on a play?

WILLIAM DARBY I could write one.

CORNELIUS WATKINS You?

WILLIAM DARBY Let's see. What does King Charles like? Bear baiting.

PHILLIP HOWARD Heathenish entertainment.

WILLIAM DARBY We make King Charles a bear, played by you. And his servant is a colonist, a cub, played by one Phillip Howard.

PHILLIP HOWARD Wait a minute.

WILLIAM DARBY The bear and the cub will get into an argument overwhat? Not tobacco, that's too obvious.

CORNELIUS WATKINS Money.

WILLIAM DARBY Too literal. ...Not money: honey! They're arguing over who gets the honey from the hive. A big scuffle ensues.

PHILLIP HOWARD And the cub takes the bear down with his skiff pole.

WILLIAM DARBY Better: the cub ends up baiting the bear.

PHILLIP HOWARD Oh that's good! And King Charles likes bear baiting! That's– what's that called?

WILLIAM DARBY Ironic.

PHILLIP HOWARD I like that!

WILLIAM DARBY So? What say you?

CORNELIUS WATKINS ...I play the bear?

PHILLIP HOWARD And I play the cub.

WILLIAM DARBY And I'll write the play.

CORNELIUS WATKINS ...Where would we perform it?

WILLIAM DARBY How about right here? If Thomas Fowkes' Tavern is good enough for the Court it's certainly good enough for the theatre. What say you Thomas Fowkes?

THOMAS FOWKES You want to stage a play here?

WILLIAM DARBY Do you mind?

THOMAS FOWKES The Court pays a fee for the use of the place.

WILLIAM DARBY We don't have any budget. This is theatre. It's for the benefit of the community. Cornelius Watkins is not the only man on the Eastern Shore hurting from the Trade Laws. And something must be done!

THOMAS FOWKES I could be taken to Court if someone complained.

WILLIAM DARBY You'll sell a lot of beer.

THOMAS FOWKES Okay.

THEY shake hands.

PHILLIP HOWARD Now wait a minute. He is right. It is blasphemy.

WILLIAM DARBY The truth is never blasphemy, Phillip Howard.

PHILLIP HOWARD Are you sure about that?

WILLIAM DARBY Cornelius Watkins, would you consider the Trade Law that reduced your tobacco to pennies, turned a county-wide bumper crop into a glut, and knocked you down from wealth to poverty in one year's time an ungodly injustice?

CORNELIUS WATKINS That is the truth!

WILLIAM DARBY Indeed. And the blasphemy belongs to Charles The Second of England, a bear of a king, who shalt not stand on the neck of his cubs any longer.

CORNELIUS WATKINS No he will not!

WILLIAM DARBY Then we're agreed!

CORNELIUS WATKINS Agreed!

WILLIAM DARBY Phillip Howard?

PHILLIP HOWARD Agreed!

WILLIAM DARBY A toast, courtesy of Thomas Fowkes! To ye bear, and ye cub. Let the baiting begin!

> *THEY cheer, toast and drink. JOHN FAWSETT enters in time to see them.*

JOHN FAWSETT Well! This is a merry lot.

PHILLIP HOWARD *(sotto voce)* Sheriff Fawsett!

WILLIAM DARBY Hello / Sheriff Fawsett.

CORNELIUS WATKINS Afternoon John Sheriff.

THOMAS FOWKES Hello John.

JOHN FAWSETT Thomas. What do we raise a glass to today, neighbors?

WILLIAM DARBY We're just celebrating Cornelius Watkins' freedom from the bonds of business.

JOHN FAWSETT You're feeling better about your change of fortune, then, Cornelius.

CORNELIUS WATKINS God has a plan for us all, brother Fawsett.

JOHN FAWSETT God does.

PHILLIP HOWARD Well, best I get back to Mister Prichard's. I'm a tenant hand for Daniel Prichard now.

JOHN FAWSETT Are you, Phillip. Daniel Prichard is doing well indeed. Why is he not here to raise a glass with you?

WILLIAM DARBY He has furniture to build for his new house.

CORNELIUS WATKINS Aak!

WILLIAM DARBY On his new plot.

CORNELIUS WATKINS Aak!

> *WILLIAM DARBY pats CORNELIUS WATKINS on the back.*

WILLIAM DARBY Speaking of new plots.

PHILLIP HOWARD Right, so I'm off! Good day Gentlemen. God willing.

> *PHILLIP HOWARD hurries out.*

ALL Good day, God bless, Amen, etc.

WILLIAM DARBY I'll be on my way as well. My quill and ink are calling me. Good day, Mister Fowkes. Sheriff Fawsett.

> *WILLIAM DARBY exits. Now alone, CORNELIUS WATKINS feels*

awkward.

CORNELIUS WATKINS I'll go too. John.

CORNELIUS WATKINS exits.

JOHN FAWSETT Good day Gentleman. ...You'd think I was a Dutch flea.

THOMAS FOWKES May I pour you anything, Sheriff Fawsett?

JOHN FAWSETT God bless you for it, Thomas.

THOMAS FOWKES obliges JOHN FAWSETT with a beer, and JOHN FAWSETT produced a packet in return.

JOHN FAWSETT And for your trouble, I have the Court's monthly payment.

THOMAS FOWKES takes it.

THOMAS FOWKES I thank you.

JOHN FAWSETT You have never once counted that purse, that I have seen.

THOMAS FOWKES I know you to be a fair man, John.

JOHN FAWSETT You're a man of integrity yourself.

THOMAS FOWKES And I know where you work.

JOHN FAWSETT Indeed.

JOHN FAWSETT toasts to that and takes a sip.

JOHN FAWSETT Ah. Any interesting talk in the tavern lately? Just now, for example?

THOMAS FOWKES Nothing that would surprise you. Cornelius Watkins having more than his share to say about the new Trade Law.

JOHN FAWSETT One cannot blame the man. He gambled everything and lost as much. God brings justice to us all in the end.

THOMAS FOWKES He does.

JOHN FAWSETT To God.

JOHN FAWSETT has lifted his glass. THOMAS FOWKES stares neutrally.

JOHN FAWSETT I know. You won't mind that I drink alone.

THOMAS FOWKES If I did I wouldn't make much of a tavern keeper.

JOHN FAWSETT drinks to that.

JOHN FAWSETT Well: I'll not keep you. You have your payment. And if there is indeed nothing of interest on the wind?

THOMAS FOWKES Another day in Pungoteague, far as I can tell.
JOHN FAWSETT Good day to you then.
THOMAS FOWKES Good day to you John.

JOHN FAWSETT exits.

Scene Seven

Music. The creek. EDWARD MARTIN is standing along the shore. THOMAS FOWKES approaches on a small wooden skiff, driving it with a pole.

EDWARD MARTIN Evening Friend.
THOMAS FOWKES Evening. I'll not trouble thee long. For Mister Smith.

THOMAS FOWKES tosses EDWARD MARTIN the purse of money that John Fawsett had given him.

EDWARD MARTIN He'll thank thee for it, as always.
THOMAS FOWKES Let him know I'll not be at the next Meeting.
EDWARD MARTIN Why is that, Friend Fowkes?
THOMAS FOWKES Best to keep my attendance irregular, for the greater good. Times what they are, Sheriff Fawsett has been around more often. Asking more questions than usual.
EDWARD MARTIN Of thee?
THOMAS FOWKES Nea, not I. Nor us. Asking after gossip.
EDWARD MARTIN Those Puritans are ever hungry for gossip.
THOMAS FOWKES John Fawsett is fair. He has a job to do is all.
EDWARD MARTIN Aye, protecting those shut up in unbelief while the rest of us can rot outside their justice.
THOMAS FOWKES Art thou want for protection, Edward Martin? Give that purse to Mister Smith and thou art safe another month at least.
EDWARD MARTIN The truth of thy faith eludes me, Thomas Fowkes. I wonder at it.
THOMAS FOWKES Don't trouble yourself.
EDWARD MARTIN Why trouble THY self, friend Fowkes, if not to the very depths of thy belief? Anything less is unworthy.
THOMAS FOWKES It's true what they say of thee.
EDWARD MARTIN Who?
THOMAS FOWKES Oh, William Darby, Cornelius Watkins, Phillip Howard.
EDWARD MARTIN Phillip Howard?

THOMAS FOWKES Those three were in the tavern today. Phillip Howard made mention of a scuffle he had here with thee?

EDWARD MARTIN Phillip Howard is a thief.

THOMAS FOWKES As art thou, so sayeth Phillip Howard.

EDWARD MARTIN I be no thief, Friend. Mark it. Phillip Howard is a lazy, sloppy ferret. What other lies did he and his brood level against me?

THOMAS FOWKES No lies that I'm aware of. Don't rile yourself over them. Anyway, you might be thanking them soon.

EDWARD MARTIN For what?

THOMAS FOWKES Tis secret for now. Mind you keep it so. But they intend to put on a play at the tavern against King Charles and the Trade Law.

EDWARD MARTIN A play? At the tavern? You would allow such a thing?

THOMAS FOWKES It will sell a good amount of beer, I think, which doesn't do us any harm, as that purse attests.

EDWARD MARTIN throws the purse back at THOMAS FOWKES.

EDWARD MARTIN Take thy purse! I'll not bear it further. It carries a sin against integrity. A sin against God.

THOMAS FOWKES Maybe God in His wisdom is more practical than thou art, Edward Martin.

EDWARD MARTIN It's the devil's money. Always has been. It's bad enough we depend on drunkenness and lawyers. Now you want us to depend on actors as well? Keep your unholy money. We don't need it.

THOMAS FOWKES In fact, we do.

THOMAS FOWKES punctuates this point by throwing the purse back.

THOMAS FOWKES Thine own prayers depend on it, Friend. Take that purse to Mister Smith. Tell him I regret that I will miss the coming Meeting. And tell him my reason as I told it thee, without your embellish/ments.

EDWARD MARTIN Aye, aye. ...One day we will be free to worship as we please.

THOMAS FOWKES One day we will. Until then, God will forgive us leaning on necessity a bit more than we favor. I do what is necessary for the true faith, Friend. Remember it. Thou wilt have thy freedom. We all will. But it won't come to us free. So until they allow us, let them pay for us. ...Evening to you Friend.

THOMAS FOWKES floats off. EDWARD MARTIN exits with the purse.

Scene Eight

TRYAL PORE and WILLIAM DARBY in the barn on the Pore property.

TRYAL PORE Tell me again, was I really convincing?

WILLIAM DARBY You saw the congregation.

TRYAL PORE I heard them all about me. But when I think back on it I see only a blur, I was swept so by my own delivery.

WILLIAM DARBY It was well done.

TRYAL PORE Thank you. And well phrased.

WILLIAM DARBY Thank you.

TRYAL PORE You can thank me with a kiss if you please. It will be my reward. Or as my mother would have it, our reward. But I won't mind sharing it with you. ...Father is at the harbor and Mother is up to her elbows in flour and water. We'll not be discovered. I am too fond of you William Darby.

WILLIAM DARBY You are. I fear I am too fond of you.

TRYAL PORE Not too, as of yet.

WILLIAM DARBY You move me, Tryal Pore.

TRYAL PORE You move me, William Darby.

...TRYAL PORE kisses WILLIAM DARBY. It's a good one. THEY look at each other.

TRYAL PORE There! We've done it! We've kissed! I don't suppose it would be practical to go any further!

WILLIAM DARBY Not likely.

TRYAL PORE Why do you resist me? If you WERE too fond of me I think you wouldn't. I know it's not your fear of God. What is it then?

WILLIAM DARBY I am too fond of you, Tryal Pore. And fornication is a punishable crime. Let those two truths suffice.

TRYAL PORE It's your independence you're too fond of, I think, not me.

WILLIAM DARBY ...I will share with you a secret.

TRYAL PORE What is it?

WILLIAM DARBY Can I trust you with it?

TRYAL PORE What is it?

WILLIAM DARBY I was in Fowkes' Tavern yesterday with Cornelius Watkins and Phillip Howard. Cornelius Watkins has been in a perpetual stir over the loss of his acres, which he has recently sold by necessity to Daniel Prichard.

TRYAL PORE The practical Carpenter.

WILLIAM DARBY I think Cornelius would take on His Majesty's fleet himself if it meant an end to the Trade Law. But he's all talk and not much ever came of that. So I suggested I write a play in satire of King Charles, and we put it on in Fowkes' Tavern.

TRYAL PORE And will you?

WILLIAM DARBY I have already begun setting word to paper.

TRYAL PORE Oh! Who will be the actors?

WILLIAM DARBY Cornelius Watkins will play King Charles in the form of a bear, and Phillip Howard will play a colonist in the form of a cub, and they will get to fighting over honey.

TRYAL PORE Oo! And who is to play the bee?

WILLIAM DARBY The bee?

TRYAL PORE The bee that makes the honey!

WILLIAM DARBY I hadn't thought of a bee.

TRYAL PORE There must be a bee. And if there is a bee seen making the honey, then the honey has been stolen by the cub. I suppose then the bee would be, what, an indentured servant. Or maybe an Indian!

WILLIAM DARBY Mmm, that gets us into another message entirely. This is to be a satire of King Charles.

TRYAL PORE Shall I play the cub then?

WILLIAM DARBY Shall you?

TRYAL PORE If there is no bee, I shall play the cub.

WILLIAM DARBY Phillip Howard plays the cub.

TRYAL PORE Is he a good actor?

WILLIAM DARBY He is not an actor that I am aware of.

TRYAL PORE I acted very well this Sabbath last.

WILLIAM DARBY Tryal Pore, it is blasphemy enough we are doing a play at all without bringing a woman into it.

TRYAL PORE You are neither too fond nor too free, but too practical by far. Who was it said to me, "Rebellion must not be too careful, lest it miss its mark for sake of fear."

WILLIAM DARBY Don't throw my words at me.

TRYAL PORE Better to throw them, I think, than only toss them about like you do.

WILLIAM DARBY I'll not have your feedback, woman.

TRYAL PORE I'll not have your not having, man.

WILLIAM DARBY and TRYAL PORE tackle one another with and in the straw. Just when the tackle risks getting sexy, CONSTANCE PORE is heard calling:

CONSTANCE PORE Tryal? Mister Darby?

TRYAL PORE It's mother.

WILLIAM DARBY Gather yourself. And not a word about the play.

TRYAL PORE I'm not stupid.

CONSTANCE PORE enters.

CONSTANCE PORE There you are. How is our student coming along, Mister Darby?

WILLIAM DARBY Very well.

CONSTANCE PORE Fine. Is the lesson nearly finished for today?

TRYAL PORE Not quite finished, Mother.

CONSTANCE PORE I am up to my elbows in flour and water and getting no help from our Sarah, lazy thing. May I ask you join me? My apologies, Mister Darby.

WILLIAM DARBY Not at all, Goody Pore. I think Tryal has had her fill of me for today. Next Tuesday then?

CONSTANCE PORE Fine.

TRYAL PORE Next Tuesday then.

WILLIAM DARBY Good day, ladies.

CONSTANCE PORE Good day Mister Darby. God be with you.

WILLIAM DARBY You as well. Good day.

WILLIAM DARBY exits. CONSTANCE PORE continues to look after him.

CONSTANCE PORE Tryal, take that straw out of your hair. I am placing my trust in the assumption that your lessons with Mister Darby are limited to reading.

TRYAL PORE Your trust is well placed.

CONSTANCE PORE As you said yourself, another confession so soon would weigh quite heavily.

TRYAL PORE I have done nothing worth confessing mother. It's the truth.

CONSTANCE PORE turns to her daughter, relieved.

CONSTANCE PORE Well. Good. Mm-hm. May I have your help with the baking then. Your father is expected soon.

TRYAL PORE I'll gather myself and come after you.

CONSTANCE PORE Good then. Very well. Alright. God bless us.

CONSTANCE PORE leaves. TRYAL PORE thinks on her mother's

protracted nervousness. TRYAL PORE *sings:*

TRYAL PORE (*sings*)
It is not enough yet
I am your daughter
It is not enough yet
To stand up straight
I'll have had my fill
When I have picked the apple
And like the serpent
opened the gate

It is not enough yet
I bake and sew
It is not enough yet
To learn to read
I'll have had my fill
When I have held the apple
And shown the good men
Whom they can heed

It is not enough yet
I wait on his word
It is not enough yet
To kiss not tell
I'll have had my fill
When I have bit the apple
And catch the wide world
In our love spell

It is not enough yet
I have no purpose
It is not enough yet
To make no mark
I'll have had my fill
When I have thrown the apple
And scared the crows back
Into the dark

It is not enough yet
I plot in silence
It is not enough yet
That no one knows
I'll have had my fill
When I've sown the apple seed
And from the old soil
A new tree grows…

I will climb up high and higher
Red horizon blue sky bright white stars
I will stoke a fire burning brighter
Climb beyond the moon and on to Mars
Ready set!

Scene Nine

A clearing in the woods. WILLIAM DARBY, CORNELIUS WATKINS and PHILLIP HOWARD are present with their costumes and props.

WILLIAM DARBY Here is a marvelous convenient place for our rehearsal. This green plot shall be our stage, this hawthorn bush our attiring room, and we will do it in action as we will before the congregation.

PHILLIP HOWARD The congregation?

WILLIAM DARBY Of drinkers, Phillip Howard, of drinkers.

CORNELIUS WATKINS William Darby!

WILLIAM DARBY What say you, wily Watkins?

CORNELIUS WATKINS There are things in this satire that will not please. Lastly, the baiting of the bear, which the ladies will not abide.

WILLIAM DARBY The ladies will in all likely not be present.

PHILLIP HOWARD No ladies?

WILLIAM DARBY In the tavern?

PHILLIP HOWARD Lizzie Crackborn came to the tavern now and again.

WILLIAM DARBY My point.

PHILLIP HOWARD Oh, right. So no ladies then.

WILLIAM DARBY Well, one never knows – ours being a rare occasion and as such bound to catch interest.

CORNELIUS WATKINS Women aside, what say you to the bear baiting? I think it is too graphic.

PHILLIP HOWARD You just don't like being seen bested by a cub.

CORNELIUS WATKINS I am thinking in consideration of our public, Phillip Howard.

WILLIAM DARBY Do not underestimate our public. They are carnivores. Their appetite for blood is not want of a good stomach. But if you like I may insert a prologue that says you yourself are not a bear and no bear was harmed, thus satisfying both those who lack imagination and those in need of reassurance, of which there are always a few.

CORNELIUS WATKINS Fine.

PHILLIP HOWARD I have a question.

WILLIAM DARBY Ask it.

PHILLIP HOWARD Given we change our rehearsal place each meeting to avoid notice, and given that, even so, three neighbors to date have asked me after our doings, and if three are asking we can wager at least a good many more are whispering; well, I just wonder at the good sense of this endeavor.

WILLIAM DARBY What you are referring to, Phillip Howard, is called word of mouth. And it is a good thing.

PHILLIP HOWARD But what of the ungodliness of it? And bear baiting is a heathenish sport to depict.

WILLIAM DARBY We are baiting no bear. We are baiting Cornelius Watkins. That I am aware, neither God nor his spokesmen have proclaimed any law against the baiting of Cornelius Watkins.

PHILLIP HOWARD You know my meaning, William Darby.

WILLIAM DARBY As you know our purpose. The Trade Law is an unjust, unbearable, ungodly hardship assailed upon us from across the sea and it must be capsized.

CORNELIUS WATKINS Yes!

WILLIAM DARBY We are but enacting the sentiments our neighbors share, and I think they will thank us not condemn us for it, despite our means of protest.

PHILLIP HOWARD Maybe.

WILLIAM DARBY That maybe must be, on Sabbath next. So come, and rehearse your parts. Bear, you begin. Cub, when he has spoke your cue, enter through that bush, and so on.

CORNELIUS WATKINS Where are we starting?

WILLIAM DARBY "But where hath my honey gone?"

CORNELIUS WATKINS "But where hath my honey gone?"

PHILLIP HOWARD May I have a moment first, to review my role.

WILLIAM DARBY Have you yet not memorized it?

PHILLIP HOWARD I work all week.

WILLIAM DARBY Take your moment. We'll wait. Cornelius, review your actions.

> *The ACTORS set to reviewing their parts. WILLIAM DARBY waits. TRYAL PORE sneaks in and hides behind the bushes with a fabricated pair of bee wings and eyes in hand.*

TRYAL PORE *(aside)* What uncouth rustics have we here? They are about to play it. I'll watch, and if I see an entrance, be an actor too.

WILLIAM DARBY Ready?

PHILLIP HOWARD Ready.

WILLIAM DARBY Very well then. Speak, Bear. Cub, stand back.

CORNELIUS WATKINS "But where hath my honey gone? Little Cub? Little Cub!"

PHILLIP HOWARD "Here, mother bear."

CORNELIUS WATKINS I have a question.

WILLIAM DARBY Ask it.

CORNELIUS WATKINS Why must I play a woman?

WILLIAM DARBY You don't play a woman. You play a bear.

CORNELIUS WATKINS A mother bear.

WILLIAM DARBY Yes: not a woman.

CORNELIUS WATKINS Why not a father bear?

WILLIAM DARBY You represent the mother country.

CORNELIUS WATKINS I thought I represented King Charles.

WILLIAM DARBY King CHARLES represents the mother country. Therefore King Charles IS the mother country, and the bear the mother bear. Anyway it's funnier if you play it as a woman.

CORNELIUS WATKINS I thought you said a mother bear!

WILLIAM DARBY Yes, a mother bear; in any case, a female. And a man playing a female is always funny.

CORNELIUS WATKINS I don't see the sense of it.

PHILLIP HOWARD You just don't like being seen as a female bested by a cub.

CORNELIUS WATKINS I am thinking in consideration of our public.

WILLIAM DARBY Speak it again, mother bear. Cub, stand back.

CORNELIUS WATKINS "But where hath my honey gone? Little Cub? Little Cub!"

PHILLIP HOWARD "Here, mother bear."

CORNELIUS WATKINS shrugs mock-helplessly.

CORNELIUS WATKINS I don't see the sense of it.

WILLIAM DARBY Would you just speak the lines!

THEY continue, and the staging takes every opportunity for slapstick it can muster.

CORNELIUS WATKINS "But where hath my honey gone? Little Cub? Little Cub!"

PHILLIP HOWARD "Here, mother bear."

CORNELIUS WATKINS "Ah! Bring my honey hither!"

PHILLIP HOWARD "But it is not your honey."

CORNELIUS WATKINS "What say you? Not my honey?"

PHILLIP HOWARD "Did you jar it?"

CORNELIUS WATKINS "No–"

PHILLIP HOWARD "Did you spin it?"

CORNELIUS WATKINS "No–"

PHILLIP HOWARD "Did you harvest it?"

CORNELIUS WATKINS "No–"

> TRYAL PORE *leaps forth, wearing her wings and bee eyes, and snatches the honey from the cub as the bear has been attempting unsuccessfully to do. The* MEN *are quite startled.*

TRYAL PORE "Did you make it? No! Did you gather the nectar? No! Did you fly from flower to flower? No! I did!"

PHILLIP HOWARD Who are you?

WILLIAM DARBY Tryal Pore!

TRYAL PORE "I am the bee!"

WILLIAM DARBY Tryal Pore, what are you doing here?

TRYAL PORE I'm playing the bee.

WILLIAM DARBY You are not playing the bee!

CORNELIUS WATKINS When did you add a bee?

WILLIAM DARBY I never added a bee. There is no bee.

TRYAL PORE "Then where did this honey come from?"

CORNELIUS WATKINS Oh! Let me play the bee!

WILLIAM DARBY There is no bee! Hand me that honey!

PHILLIP HOWARD Who told you where to find us?

TRYAL PORE Nobody told me. I tracked you on my own.

WILLIAM DARBY The honey, Tryal Pore!

PHILLIP HOWARD You see? We've been discovered! And by a woman! You said there would be no women!

WILLIAM DARBY Phillip Howard, calm yourself. She's come alone and I am sure she hasn't told anyone, have you!

TRYAL PORE I'm not stupid.

PHILLIP HOWARD She doesn't have to tell anyone for it to reach God's own ear. No doubt he's been listening all along. He hears everything! I'm through with this play. It's dangerous.

TRYAL PORE I'll play the cub!

WILLIAM DARBY No you will not. Phillip Howard is playing the cub. Phillip Howard, you put those ears back on right now!

CORNELIUS WATKINS Let me play the cub!

WILLIAM DARBY Shut it, mother bear! Phillip Howard?

PHILLIP HOWARD No.

WILLIAM DARBY We are performing this play and to that end you will put those cub ears on your head and rehearse this scene, now do it!

CORNELIUS WATKINS I'll do it! Give me the ears!

PHILLIP HOWARD No.

CORNELIUS WATKINS If you won't play the cub I will, and William Darby shall play the bear!

WILLIAM DARBY (to TRYAL PORE) See what you've done?

TRYAL PORE What's the matter? Bee in your bonnet?

WILLIAM DARBY Give me that. Phillip Howard!

> *WILLIAM DARBY has snatched the honey from TRYAL PORE and tossed it to PHILLIP HOWARD, who catches it.*
>
> *In that instant CORNELIUS WATKINS manages to nab PHILLIP HOWARD'S cub ears.*

PHILLIP HOWARD Ahp!

> *PHILLIP HOWARD likewise manages to snatch his cub ears back and don them. CORNELIUS WATKINS goes after PHILLIP HOWARD.*

WILLIAM DARBY Buzz off little bee! Cornelius Watkins, put on your head! Get that honey!

> *Music. CORNELIUS WATKINS flips his bear head back on and goes after PHILLIP HOWARD. TRYAL PORE claps and bounces about as WILLIAM DARBY continues to corral the squabbling bear and cub.*
>
> *Scene transforms to...*

Scene Ten

> *Fowkes' Tavern, packed. EVERYONE is there, it seems, and they are cheering on the cub vociferously.*

> CORNELIUS WATKINS *continues to pursue PHILLIP HOWARD, who eventually manages to bait him to a pole and slaughter him violently, ripping heaps of red yarn from the bear's bowels. The CROWD goes wild with joyful blood lust.*
>
> CORNELIUS WATKINS *dies a protracted death. The end.*

WILLIAM DARBY Hey!

> *The CROWD takes up WILLIAM DARBY'S cheer and applaud enthusiastically. PHILLIP HOWARD and CORNELIUS WATKINS take their bows. The show is a hit and EVERYONE is buzzing, raising glasses, clapping the artists on the back, etc.*
>
> *Outside the tavern, EDWARD MARTIN listens and seethes. After a moment of this, EDWARD MARTIN looks up to God. HE closes his eyes and prays in silence, his hands open. The music hums while he does.*
>
> *TRYAL PORE notices EDWARD MARTIN at a distance. The tavern and its CROWD seem to recede.*
>
> *Finally, EDWARD MARTIN closes his hands, then opens his eyes again, looking out into the night, his mind at work.*

TRYAL PORE *(sings)*
I have an eye on this town
Got my ear to the ground
This is a new song
It's not finished yet
The ending is only temporary
How its course will run
I'm not taking bets

> *EDWARD MARTIN exits. TRYAL PORE exits.*

Intermission

Act Two
Scene Eleven

> *In the barn on the Pore property. TRYAL PORE is kissing WILLIAM DARBY madly and playfully. Then:*

TRYAL PORE Oo! Next you shall write a grand, romantic comedy and I shall play the heroine.

WILLIAM DARBY A GRAND romantic comedy. Is there such a thing? There are grand romantic TRAGEDIES.

TRYAL PORE Yes but who wants a tragic romance?

WILLIAM DARBY Nobody wants one, but they frequently have them.

TRYAL PORE Well I shall play in a grand, sweeping, spectacular romantic COMEDY – with music – and if such a thing did not exist before, it will now. A new genre for the New World. You will write it, and it will be done across the colonies – now that you're a famous playwright.

WILLIAM DARBY Infamous.

TRYAL PORE There was no scandal. Even my Father and Mother were roused quite favorably to the occasion.

WILLIAM DARBY We served a public need to purge its discontent. We were more than practical. We had purpose. And this is why I shall not write your grand, sweeping, spectacular romantic comedy with music.

TRYAL PORE I don't really want you to write it. I want you to live it – with me.

WILLIAM DARBY Tryal, when we performed the play, and all our neighbors rallied themselves to a frenzy, I felt my old life surging back to me from across the sea. That's how it was. We were actors and thieves, and we were doing things that mattered – mattered so much that Cromwell wanted to hang us all. That night in Fowkes' Tavern was not just a little comedy about a bear and cub squabbling over honey. It was a community event. It meant something. Since I arrived on this Eastern Shore I have done nothing but keep ledgers, draft business letters, teach children to read.

TRYAL PORE Children!

WILLIAM DARBY The only thing I've been able to call mine was my freedom, which I thought I had. But truly I've only been pacing back and forth between other men's busy work. When that tavern exploded, I felt again what freedom really is. Not practicality. Purpose.

TRYAL PORE I felt that too. And I want it too. With you.

WILLIAM DARBY I am with you.

TRYAL PORE In a barn. In secret.

WILLIAM DARBY ...I am still dangerously fond of you, Tryal Pore. But something changed in the tavern. I need to understand it.

TRYAL PORE ...So do I. Soon. I may be a child who needs tutoring in God's Good Book. But I understand who I am. And I won't be able to wait much longer for you to understand.

WILLIAM DARBY reaches for TRYAL PORE's hair and she smacks his hand.

TRYAL PORE ...Next Tuesday then?

WILLIAM DARBY ...Next Tuesday then.

WILLIAM DARBY leaves.

Music.

TRYAL PORE No I don't want to sing.

The music stops. It starts again. TRYAL PORE still does not wish to sing.

Scene Twelve

Fowkes' Tavern. THOMAS FOWKES, EDMOND PORE and JOHN FAWSETT have gathered there.

EDMOND PORE Thank you for meeting with us, Thomas.

THOMAS FOWKES My doors are always open to you, Edmond, as you know. John.

EDMOND PORE Something has arisen in regard to the openness of these doors.

THOMAS FOWKES What's that?

EDMOND PORE Edward Martin, a longtime indentured servant on the property of Robert Smith, has brought charges against William Darby, Cornelius Watkins and Phillip Howard.

THOMAS FOWKES Has he?

JOHN FAWSETT For blasphemy.

EDMOND PORE I don't imagine Edward Martin has ever paid his respects in your tavern, but those who DO know him would tell you Edward Martin has had a thorn in his side since birth.

JOHN FAWSETT This isn't the first time he's brought a charge of Blasphemy. Not that any have gone through.

EDMOND PORE The Court has more important matters to contend with than Edward Martin's spleen. Still, a play should not have been allowed. But it spoke the community's mind and no one seemed disquieted, Martin excepted. Out of respect for the general temperament this hard season, I would throw the charge aside were it not that word of Mister Darby, Watkins and Howard's act has reached Jamestown. A Major Howell Cross of His Majesty's Council Appointed to Foreign Plantations has expressed his interest in the matter, and intends a visit. And so I am afraid the case must be pursued.

THOMAS FOWKES Why not dismiss it as rumor? Maybe they only intended to do it.

JOHN FAWSETT Too many witnesses, Thomas. The tavern was packed, as you know.

EDMOND PORE Rule of law is crucial to the strength and social fabric of this colony. Otherwise we're no better than the savages that surround us. As authority of the Accomack County Court and Harbor Captain in His Majesty's fleet, I am responsible, alongside Sheriff Fawsett, for the order of this community – which as you know is of no small economic significance, and of no small interest to either side of the Atlantic. ...Did you have to let them do it on the Sabbath, Thomas?

THOMAS FOWKES Nobody missed their Church. The play was performed after services.

JOHN FAWSETT The Sabbath is the Sabbath, at any hour.

THOMAS FOWKES Gentlemen. It will not do for my place of business to be publicly notarized a place of sin. Besides, I have often served on the Sabbath.

EDMOND PORE We are well aware of that, Thomas. A great many cases against your patrons for breaking the Sabbath have passed through this court, though we have never yet charged you for it.

THOMAS FOWKES Never yet? If you do it, Edmond, it will be complicated for everyone. I don't imagine this Major Cross from Jamestown would smile upon a court that knowingly holds session in a Sabbath-breaking tavern. Neither would it help the judge of such a Court in taking any steps himself toward Jamestown.

EDMOND PORE I beg your pardon!

JOHN FAWSETT He's right, Edmond.

EDMOND PORE ...You're a plain-spoken man, Thomas Fowkes. I won't argue it.

THOMAS FOWKES Don't bring Darby, Watkins and Howard on charges of Blasphemy. Let that pass if it will. Put your eye on the play – that's violation enough – but leave the day of the week to God and the calendar.

JOHN FAWSETT The play WAS a slander against King Charles. The charge could be sedition.

THOMAS FOWKES Yes. And in the end isn't sedition what matters most to Jamestown? Edward Martin may have cared to charge Blasphemy, but you can't tell me this Major Cross, when he comes, won't be thirsty on any given day he likes. If King Charles ever paid a visit, I'm sure he'd be thirsty too. Let Sunday go. The play's the thing.

Music.

EDMOND PORE ...This must go well. We cannot afford to lose the sympathy of our neighbors – in Pungoteague, Jamestown, or London. The order must be maintained. ...John?

JOHN FAWSETT I'll draw up the warrants.

EDMOND PORE God help us.

> *EDMOND PORE and JOHN FAWSETT exit. THOMAS FOWKES' mind is busy, and he exits as well.*

Scene Thirteen

> *Music. The creek. EDWARD MARTIN is standing along the shore. THOMAS FOWKES approaches on a small wooden skiff, driving it with a pole.*

EDWARD MARTIN Evening Friend.

THOMAS FOWKES Do you do any work at all, Edward Martin, or do you just stand here waiting for trouble to float by?

EDWARD MARTIN What brings thee up creek, Friend Fowkes?

THOMAS FOWKES I think you know what.

EDWARD MARTIN Thou hast heard of my charge, then. Has it been brought?

THOMAS FOWKES John Fawsett is drawing up the warrants. Darby, Watkins and Howard are to be charged with acting a seditious play.

EDWARD MARTIN And blasphemy.

THOMAS FOWKES No, Friend. Acting a seditious play, and only that.

EDWARD MARTIN I told Sheriff Fawsett blasphemy. They did not only act a play, they acted it on God's holy day, to a crowd of drunkards who should have been thanking the Lord their savior, not Darby, Watkins and Phillip Coward.

THOMAS FOWKES Did it occur to you, Edward Martin, that for housing that play I might be counted among your accused? What if the tavern were closed? Where would the Friends get their money? Did it further occur to you that by making charges you would then have to make your case, in the Court, where you would be asked to take an oath of allegiance to the Crown and swear upon a King James Bible?

EDWARD MARTIN I would not do either, for certain.

THOMAS FOWKES Yes, thus announcing yourself Quaker, and putting me and every other Friend who gathers under Mister Smith's roof in danger of the same. Did you think of that? ...You would do well to give more consideration before you bark, Friend. ...Well? What say you?

EDWARD MARTIN ...What should I do?

THOMAS FOWKES You beg that question too late but I'll give you an answer, beggar. When the day comes, you stay standing right there and pray no more trouble comes floating back to you. You didn't actually SEE the play yourself, so you have nothing but hearsay to testify anyway. But if you don't show the case might be dismissed. When it is, I'll come let you know. Until then I think it best we not meet here. Tell Mister Smith I'll not be joining the Meetings for a time. And tell him why.
EDWARD MARTIN I will. I thank thee, Friend Fowkes.
THOMAS FOWKES Keep your thanks, and your mouth shut. ...You have set a thing in motion, Edward Martin. God help us.

> *THOMAS FOWKES floats off. EDWARD MARTIN looks up to God, then hurries away.*

Scene Fourteen

> *Outside the former home of CORNELIUS WATKINS, now belonging to DANIEL PRICHARD. Both men are there, along with PHILLIP HOWARD, seated and eating or drinking. WILLIAM DARBY arrives.*

WILLIAM DARBY Good day, gentlemen.
OTHERS Darby! William Darby! Good day. Etc.
CORNELIUS WATKINS Well timed as always, William Darby; Mister Prichard has just broken us to dinner.
DANIEL PRICHARD Take a plate and a chair, Mister Darby?
WILLIAM DARBY Thank you I will. I don't remember your having so many chairs and plates when this was your plot, Cornelius Watkins.
CORNELIUS WATKINS Shut it.
PHILLIP HOWARD The chairs we built. The plates we carved.
WILLIAM DARBY Mister Prichard keeps his hands busy.
CORNELIUS WATKINS Indeed.
DANIEL PRICHARD The roof on Mister Watkins' new cabin is coming along. Isn't it Mister Watkins?
CORNELIUS WATKINS We'll see if it leaks come winter.

> *Good natured laughter.*

DANIEL PRICHARD What brings you, Mister Darby?
WILLIAM DARBY Haven't seen the troupe in some time and thought I'd inquire how life has treated them since our debut.
PHILLIP HOWARD I've gained the attention of a lady or two. Of course, they only want me for my honey.

Naughty laughter.

CORNELIUS WATKINS   All I've gained are blisters working Mister Prichard's wood.

Oh! Boo!

PHILLIP HOWARD   Oh! Listen to him. He can't make a run into town without coming home with a skiff-load of compliments. What number of times is it now you've been asked to do a bit of mama bear?

CORNELIUS WATKINS   I don't keep track.

DANIEL PRICHARD   You said thirty-six this morning.

CORNELIUS WATKINS   Thirty-seven.

The OTHERS laugh.

WILLIAM DARBY   I haven't lacked for appreciative nods myself. I've been thinking another outing may be in order.

PHILLIP HOWARD   Another play?

WILLIAM DARBY   The Trade Law is still in effect, is it not? We're still paying taxes to keep London's bridges up, are we not? There is plenty for ye bear and ye cub to growl about, and an audience eager to growl along. We're popular. Best to capitalize on it while we can.

DANIEL PRICHARD   Mister Darby is right. Popularity is a fickle gift. Not practical in the long run.

WILLIAM DARBY   One doesn't make a life in the theatre for practical reasons, Mister Prichard.

DANIEL PRICHARD   I do not doubt it. Land, a home, a good wife and family, and God's green earth. That will see you through. God's green earth is a given; now that I have the land and the home, all I need is a good wife.

PHILLIP HOWARD   Any prospects?

DANIEL PRICHARD   Oh. I've been a bit busy here with you gentlemen.

CORNELIUS WATKINS   That's a no, then.

Laughter.

DANIEL PRICHARD   I have time. I'll find her. And the rest will follow.

WILLIAM DARBY   Nevertheless, you wouldn't mind your tenant hands doing a little impractical rehearsing for a popular cause on their own time, would you Mister Prichard?

DANIEL PRICHARD   Not I. But I can't speak for God.

WILLIAM DARBY   I imagine God favors justice more than anyone. That's what we're in it for in the end.

DANIEL PRICHARD And popularity?

WILLIAM DARBY An added bonus. What say you, troupe?

PHILLIP HOWARD I'm in.

CORNELIUS WATKINS I suppose I wouldn't mind.

PHILLIP HOWARD You can hardly wait for thirty-eight.

WILLIAM DARBY Good then. Now, lend your ears, that I might plant in them a seed for our next endeavor, in which Cub sneaks aboard one of Bear's ships disguised as an Indian and dumps a cargo of tobacco bound for England into the harbor.

Appreciative vocal reaction.

PHILLIP HOWARD Oh, that's good!

CORNELIUS WATKINS What is Bear dressed as?

WILLIAM DARBY Ship Captain, of course.

"Hey, not bad" vocal reaction.

WILLIAM DARBY The technical challenge will be to depict the ship at sea. I had an idea / that we...

PHILLIP HOWARD and CORNELIUS WATKINS both jump in with ideas at once. The three theater-makers are brainstorming as JOHN FAWSETT enters. DANIEL PRICHARD is the first to see him.

DANIEL PRICHARD Sheriff Fawsett!

JOHN FAWSETT Good day / Gentlemen.

DARBY, WATKINS AND HOWARD Oh! Good day, Sheriff Fawsett. Etc.

DANIEL PRICHARD Take a plate and a chair, Sheriff?

JOHN FAWSETT That's very kind of you, Mister Prichard. But I won't be staying long.

DANIEL PRICHARD What can we do for you then?

JOHN FAWSETT I'm afraid I've come with a warrant for you three gentlemen.

CORNELIUS WATKINS A warrant?

JOHN FAWSETT Charges have been brought against you, for the acting of a seditious play.

WILLIAM DARBY Charges? Brought by who?

JOHN FAWSETT A mister Edward Martin.

PHILLIP HOWARD Edward Martin?

JOHN FAWSETT That's right.

CORNELIUS WATKINS And you accepted them, John?

JOHN FAWSETT The acting of that play was a serious violation.

WILLIAM DARBY Of what?

JOHN FAWSETT Act 1-1649, paragraph 1, denying the divine right of Kings; paragraph 2, defending proceedings that deny succession of the King; and paragraph 3, to propose a change in government, or doubt the power of the governor or government, or equally high treason.

PHILLIP HOWARD We did all that?

JOHN FAWSETT I'm afraid so.

CORNELIUS WATKINS I don't remember doing ANY of that.

JOHN FAWSETT You can say as much two weeks from today at the next Court session, to which you are all expected to report. I'll not keep you until then. But I would advise you not to commit any further theatrical acts in the meantime. It would not be practical.

WILLIAM DARBY Thank you Sheriff.

CORNELIUS WATKINS Thank you?!

WILLIAM DARBY Shut it Watkins.

JOHN FAWSETT So, unless you have any questions to put to me, I'll leave you to dinner.

WILLIAM DARBY No questions.

JOHN FAWSETT Very well. Good day then. Mister Prichard.

DANIEL PRICHARD Good day, Sheriff Fawsett.

> *JOHN FAWSETT exits. The REST stare at one another. PHILLIP HOWARD breaks the stillness by throwing down his hat.*

PHILLIP HOWARD This is the revenge of Edward Martin! Let that be the next play you write, William Darby! "The Revenge of Edward Martin!" In which Phillip Howard is sent to the scaffold for the murder of the title personae, a curmudgeon and thief!

DANIEL PRICHARD Watch your words, Phillip Howard.

PHILLIP HOWARD You know I don't mean it, Mister Prichard. But I am RILED! Edward Martin! What's going to happen? What do we do?

WILLIAM DARBY We go to court and make our case. We have the popular favor, we know it.

CORNELIUS WATKINS Will we still? Do you think our neighbors will admit to attending and revelling in a seditious play? *(a realization)* On the Sabbath!

PHILLIP HOWARD Oh, that's bad. This just got worse.

CORNELIUS WATKINS It always was. We were too busy being popular to notice. We will be condemned! Condemned!

WILLIAM DARBY Now don't panic. We will go to court, and we will state our case, on which we will confer. But we will not panic.

PHILLIP HOWARD I know! We'll reveal Edward Martin to be Quaker!

CORNELIUS WATKINS Yes!

WILLIAM DARBY No, that would not do for Thomas Fowkes, who need not be troubled in this. Nor need we address the Sabbath as it did not figure in the charge as stated.

CORNELIUS WATKINS What DO we address then?

WILLIAM DARBY As little as possible. In any case, when faced with the unexpected, an actor improvises. THIS is our next performance, gentlemen. And it must be both practical AND popular. What say you?

CORNELIUS WATKINS God help us.

PHILLIP HOWARD Amen.

WILLIAM DARBY Good then. Rehearsal starts now.

DANIEL PRICHARD Work's not done.

WILLIAM DARBY Rehearsal starts tonight.

DANIEL PRICHARD And you can use the barn.

WILLIAM DARBY Thank you, Daniel. ...Troupe?

A three-way handshake seals the matter. WILLIAM DARBY raises his free fist.

WILLIAM DARBY To ye bear and ye cub. Let the trial begin!

CORNELIUS WATKINS and PHILLIP HOWARD raise their free fists with less confidence.

Scene Fifteen

In which the trial takes place and plots thicken, as underscored, and intermittently conveyed to us lyrically, by the unholy music of TRYAL PORE.

We begin in Fowkes' Tavern, currently the court. THOMAS FOWKES and EDMOND PORE are there. MAJOR HOWELL CROSS has just arrived.

EDMOND PORE I welcome you to Pungoteague, Major Cross.

MAJOR HOWELL CROSS I thank you, Captain Pore. Please forgive my late arrival. It is a rather long journey to you.

EDMOND PORE I apologize I was unable to greet you at the Harbor myself but you see our Court schedule was quite full.

MAJOR HOWELL CROSS It seems it has emptied since.

EDMOND PORE We wait on the Darby Watkins Howard case, knowing it is of special interest to you; but also the plaintiff has not yet shown himself.

MAJOR HOWELL CROSS The plaintiff has not arrived?

EDMOND PORE Indeed no. I have just sent Sheriff Fawsett to bring the defendants, that we may at the least hear their statements and not lose the day entirely. In the meantime, if you like, we may discuss any other business you might wish to address with me while you are here.

MAJOR HOWELL CROSS I have no business here, Captain Pore, but to assure Jamestown that the Accomack County Court operates in strict covenant with His Majesty's regularly appointed Courts. Yours being, as you know, the only court in Virginia to have appointed itself prior to recognition from Jamestown makes it of unique interest.

EDMOND PORE As I once wrote to His Majesty, let our initiative be a sign of this community's devotion to maintaining order and justice in his good name, and under God.

MAJOR HOWELL CROSS Yes, I read that letter. Your county holds a reputation for its independent spirit.

EDMOND PORE Our being somewhat removed from the Colony center does present its challenges, as your long journey attests. Timeliness on occasion has necessitated prompt action. Another sign, I hope, that we do not make time for disorder here.

MAJOR HOWELL CROSS The present case seems to be in no hurry.

EDMOND PORE Well–. This plaintiff may take his case lightly, but we shall not. Do we know where Mister Martin is? Do we know?

THOMAS FOWKES I couldn't say.

MAJOR HOWELL CROSS And you are, Mister?

THOMAS FOWKES Thomas Fowkes, Sir.

MAJOR HOWELL CROSS The tavern keeper.

THOMAS FOWKES The same.

MAJOR HOWELL CROSS It is a pleasure to meet you, Mister, after so long and tiring a journey.

THOMAS FOWKES thinks he understands, and extends his hand.

THOMAS FOWKES Beer or wine, Major Cross.

But:

MAJOR HOWELL CROSS While the Court is in session?

Music.

EDMOND PORE After! After, of course.

THOMAS FOWKES Of course. I like to know the tastes of my new guests. It helps supply meet demand, when the time is due.

MAJOR HOWELL CROSS Wine then. When the time is due.

THOMAS FOWKES Very well, Sir.

EDMOND PORE Yes. Very well then.

> *TRYAL PORE steps forth with an aside, sung, during which WILLIAM DARBY, CORNELIUS WATKINS, and PHILLIP HOWARD arrive with JOHN FAWSETT and the rest of the town.*

TRYAL PORE *(sings)*
Very well Judge Edmond Pore
The stage is set; time to perform
Justice waits so watch your tongue
And wait to drink your wine 'til Jamestown is done

Now here they come, the Accomack Three
A crowd draws near, their fate to see
"Where is the plaintiff, what's the rumor, say
What have you heard? What will Judge Pore decree?"

> *The trial commences. (Music is now continuous throughout this entire scene, shifting accordingly as things progress.)*

EDMOND PORE This court is now back in session. Let it be noted the plaintiff, Edward Martin, is not present. Defendants William Darby, Cornelius Watkins, and Phillip Howard: you are charged with the crime of acting a seditious play. What say you to this?

WILLIAM DARBY It is true, Sir, we acted a play. But we did not intend with this act, nor, we maintain, did we incite with it, either harm or treason.

EDMOND PORE On this you each agree?

CORNELIUS WATKINS Yes, Sir.

PHILLIP HOWARD Yes, Sir.

WILLIAM DARBY Yes, Sir.

EDMOND PORE And your evidence?

WILLIAM DARBY ...Evidence? Why, the play itself. As you / know

EDMOND PORE –Ah–!'ave you a copy of the play written?

CORNELIUS WATKINS Your Honor, you saw / the–

EDMOND PORE –Orrr was it done extempore?

PHILLIP HOWARD What?

WILLIAM DARBY It was not improvised, no. I did write the play.

EDMOND PORE Will you provide the Court with a copy of such versus and speeches as comprised this play? For surely, not having seen it, I must read the play in order to arrive at any conclusion as to its nature. Therefore, will you provide it?

WILLIAM DARBY It may be provided, yes. I will need to fetch it.

MAJOR HOWELL CROSS Judge Pore, if I may, what of the performance itself?

EDMOND PORE I did not see it.

MAJOR HOWELL CROSS You have said. But what Mister Darby has written will not convey how it was performed. I should think we must also see the play.

EDMOND PORE See the play? In court?

MAJOR HOWELL CROSS As evidence.

EDMOND PORE ...Can you perform the play?

CORNELIUS WATKINS *(sotto voce to DARBY)* No. No. No. / No.

WILLIAM DARBY We would need to gather our habiliments. And it has been some time since the performance. We would need to rehearse.

EDMOND PORE Major Cross?

MAJOR HOWELL CROSS The true nature of the act itself must be assessed.

PHILLIP HOWARD *(to Darby)* They want us to do the play again?

WILLIAM DARBY Shut it.

EDMOND PORE Very well. Let it be ordered that the defendants, Misters Darby, Watkins and Howard, shall perform at the next Court session their play as it was executed last. It is further ordered that the plaintiff, Edward Martin, be duly informed of the preceding order, and that he too must appear to witness the performance and state his charge against it. Court is adjourned.

>   *TRYAL PORE sings as the court disperses. DANIEL PRICHARD, however, catches sight of TRYAL PORE and lingers.*

TRYAL PORE *(sings)*
Very well Judge Edmond Pore
The stage is set to wait for more
Justice was delayed, well done,
Now you can drink your wine with Jamestown; have fun

And off they went, the Accomack Three
The crowd ran home excitedly
"Can you believe it, did you hear the play
will be reprised? What will Judge Pore decree?"

And the summer can see autumn
And the waiting makes me hate 'em
If seasons can change with ease; Why not we?

DANIEL PRICHARD You must be Tryal Pore, Judge Pore's daughter.
TRYAL PORE I am.
DANIEL PRICHARD Daniel Prichard is my name.
TRYAL PORE The practical carpenter!
DANIEL PRICHARD You know me.
TRYAL PORE I've heard you mentioned somewhat.
DANIEL PRICHARD I understand you had a confession a while back, and that it went well. I regret I did not manage to see it.
TRYAL PORE That's alright. There will be others.
DANIEL PRICHARD I do hope it left you well.
TRYAL PORE I seem to have carried on well enough.
DANIEL PRICHARD May I be too forward then?
TRYAL PORE Too forward?
DANIEL PRICHARD To ask to accompany you, with your family, to the next service.
TRYAL PORE You wish to ply my father about the case.
DANIEL PRICHARD Not about the case.
TRYAL PORE What then?
DANIEL PRICHARD I may one day ply your father about you. For now, I wish to sit beside you. If I happen to do so in the church, it will cause you no rumor.
TRYAL PORE I see. Well. I will consider that, Mister Prichard.
DANIEL PRICHARD Daniel.
TRYAL PORE Daniel Prichard.

> *Staring. Finally DANIEL PRICHARD leaves. TRYAL PORES sings:*

TRYAL PORE *(sings)*
And the summer can see autumn
And the waiting makes me hate 'em
If seasons can change with ease, so might we.

> *EVERYONE gathers again for the second trial. WILLIAM DARBY watches attentively as CORNELIUS WATKINS and PHILLIP HOWARD enact the finale of the play we saw before, only this time it is a bit more restrained. The crowd is likewise more restrained.*

> *When it is done, ALL are not sure how to respond properly until MAJOR HOWELL CROSS gets the applause going, and then ALL join.*

EDMOND PORE Thank you, Gentlemen. Your evidence shall be duly considered. However, as this performance has taken up the time allotted to this case today, and since the plaintiff, Edward Martin, has once again not deigned to attend, I am afraid my verdict must be put off to yet another Court session. In consideration thereof, it is ordered that Sheriff Fawsett personally escort Mister Martin to the next court session to finally make his case. Court is adjourned.

> *The crowd disperses, gossiping madly. MAJOR HOWELL CROSS approaches EDMOND PORE.*

MAJOR HOWELL CROSS Captain Pore.

EDMOND PORE Major Cross, I must apologize for this plaintiff. This is highly unusual.

MAJOR HOWELL CROSS Indeed. I did not anticipate this case would be so protracted. I am afraid my time and duty is such that I must return to Jamestown and make my report on these proceedings before they have officially been concluded.

EDMOND PORE I assure you our proceedings here have always been noted for their efficiency. But this Edward Martin character–

MAJOR HOWELL CROSS Yes, you were quite right to summon him so tersely. No citizen must be allowed to wield the hand of Justice as he pleases.

EDMOND PORE No.

MAJOR HOWELL CROSS And as for this play.

EDMOND PORE *(shaking his head disapprovingly)* Yes.

MAJOR HOWELL CROSS It was entertaining.

EDMOND PORE ...It– It, wha–

MAJOR HOWELL CROSS I see no harm in it, nor sedition.

EDMOND PORE It, entertaining, yes–

MAJOR HOWELL CROSS To be honest I found it rather boring.

EDMOND PORE Boring. Yes. I–

MAJOR HOWELL CROSS And why was there no bee? Two bears, a jar of honey, and no bee? Clearly they are amateurs. Regardless, it IS theatre; and though His Majesty is not entirely averse to it I trust you to see the gentlemen responsible end their theatrical activities here.

EDMOND PORE Of course.

MAJOR HOWELL CROSS Well then. I am afraid I must take my leave. I thank you, Captain Pore, and bid you good day.

EDMOND PORE Well, thank you, Major Cross. One final glass before Sheriff Fawsett and I accompany you to the Harbor?

MAJOR HOWELL CROSS Very well.

> EDMOND PORE gestures JOHN FAWSETT to come along as the three of them exit the tavern. THOMAS FOWKES remains in thought for a moment.

TRYAL PORE (sings)
Very well Judge Edmond Pore
The Bears were tamed and bored the Boar
Justice was delayed, well done,
Now you can drink your wine and Jamestown is gone

> As TRYAL PORE sings, THOMAS FOWKES exits and the scene transforms to the creek.

TRYAL PORE (sings)
And off he goes, the Quaker Tom Fowkes
A change of plans and Friend to coax
Edward Martin must show in court
But in the end: what will Judge Pore decree?

> The creek. EDWARD MARTIN is standing along the shore. THOMAS FOWKES approaches on a small wooden skiff, driving it with a pole.

EDWARD MARTIN Evening Friend. How goes it in the court?

THOMAS FOWKES Not well.

EDWARD MARTIN For whom?

THOMAS FOWKES You will be receiving a visit from Sheriff Fawsett, come to summon you to the next Court session. It's best now you attend.

EDWARD MARTIN Attend? Will they ask me to take oath unto the King and swear upon their Bible?

THOMAS FOWKES I expect they will. And you will do it.

EDWARD MARTIN Friend Fowkes–

THOMAS FOWKES You are not in the Court's favor. Your case was not dismissed and your absence has not been taken kindly.

EDWARD MARTIN That was your advice, Thomas Fowkes.

THOMAS FOWKES I know it. When Sheriff Fawsett summons you, come, take oath, swear upon the Bible, accept what is decreed, say nothing contrary, and end this. That is what I think best for all.

EDWARD MARTIN What THOU think best? What good has thy best thinking done me yet?

THOMAS FOWKES This is your storm, Edward Martin. I am blowing against a wind you whipped. I will see you, well-heeled, in the Court. Good evening.

> THOMAS FOWKES leaves without delay. EDWARD MARTIN lingers a moment, while TRYAL PORE sings, before making his own exit.

TRYAL PORE *(sings)*
And the summer can see autumn
And the waiting makes us hate 'em
If seasons can change with ease; Why don't we?

> *DANIEL PRICHARD approaches TRYAL PORE, who responds expectantly.*

DANIEL PRICHARD Good day, Tryal Pore.

TRYAL PORE Good day, Mister Prichard.

DANIEL PRICHARD Have you considered of the courtesy I asked of you?

TRYAL PORE I have. You may accompany me to church, if it suits you. Though I think you need not trouble my Father or Mother with your intentions. I cannot help who happens to sit beside me from service to service.

DANIEL PRICHARD I do not wish my intentions to be a secret.

TRYAL PORE ...But you don't know me.

DANIEL PRICHARD I understand you.

TRYAL PORE You understand me? How is that?

DANIEL PRICHARD When I look on you, everything you hold inside is visible to me.

TRYAL PORE What do you see?

DANIEL PRICHARD Your honesty. Your force. Your wisdom.

TRYAL PORE You see that? Where?

DANIEL PRICHARD In the curve of your neck when you stand watching something that holds your mind. In your eyes when you are thinking intently and forget there are others near you. In your hands when you don't wish to be still any longer.

TRYAL PORE You see all that?

DANIEL PRICHARD I do.

TRYAL PORE ...I will see you in the church, Mister Prichard.

> *DANIEL PRICHARD tips his hat to TRYAL PORE and exits. TRYAL PORE sings:*

TRYAL PORE *(sings)*
And the summer will be autumn
And the waiting makes me hate 'em
If seasons can change with ease, so can we:
Like the way I said yes to a man I don't know!
Have I done wrong? Will the Lord forgive me even so?
And how will this next season go?

EVERYONE gathers again for the third trial. EDWARD MARTIN is now present and JOHN FAWSETT is presenting him with a King James Bible. EDWARD MARTIN looks at it.

JOHN FAWSETT ...Your right hand.

After another moment of hesitation, EDWARD MARTIN complies.

JOHN FAWSETT Edward Martin, do you swear your allegiance to His Majesty, the King, Charles the Second.

EDWARD MARTIN ...I do.

JOHN FAWSETT And do you swear upon this holy Bible that the evidence you give today shall be the truth, so help you God.

EDWARD MARTIN ...I swear it.

EDMOND PORE Edward Martin. This is the third court session that has been granted to the charge brought by you against the defendants. Why is it then the first time we have received the honor of your attendance?

EDWARD MARTIN I have been busier than I expected.

EDMOND PORE Busier than you expected.

EDWARD MARTIN On Mister Smith's plot.

EDMOND PORE Mister Smith's plot is one of the smaller in the County. And yet you see many neighbors who work much larger plots here with us today, among them your accused.

EDWARD MARTIN I cannot account for how hard my neighbors do or do not work.

This does not ingratiate EDWARD MARTIN to the CROWD.

EDMOND PORE Edward Martin, can you give reason why the accused should be found guilty of the charge you have brought against them.

EDWARD MARTIN They acted a play on the Sabbath. It is at least twice a blasphemy.

EDMOND PORE Can you identify the aspects of the play that offend?

EDWARD MARTIN ...I did not see it.

EDMOND PORE You did not see it.

EDWARD MARTIN It would be blasphemy to attend.

EDMOND PORE You have accused three of your neighbors of an act you did not see?

EDWARD MARTIN It is well known they performed the play, right here in this tavern.

EDMOND PORE Yes, and were you to have attended these proceedings you would have seen the play performed again, right here in this COURT. That performance was deemed innocuous by not only me but a representative of Jamestown as well. What say you to this?

EDWARD MARTIN   ...I say–

EDMOND PORE   –You will say nothing. You were not there. Therefore you have waived your right to comment. Sheriff Fawsett, let it be ordered that the defendants, William Darby, Cornelius Watkins and Phillip Howard, be acquitted of all charges brought against them in this case. Furthermore, whereas the plaintiff, Edward Martin, neglected twice to attend proceedings brought about by his accusation, and whereas the accusation was made by Mister Martin without his having actually witnessed the alleged crime itself, and for as much as it is upon Mister Martin's FRIVOLOUS accusation and trouble the suit did accrue THREE TIMES OVER, it is therefore ordered that Edward Martin pay all costs related to this suit – for himself, the defendants, and the Court.

This goes down very well with the CROWD, who all cheer EDMOND PORE's decision. The music stops.

EDMOND PORE   Edward Martin, what say you to this?

EDWARD MARTIN   I thought I was to say nothing. But if you now have given me leave to speak, I will say this. Fifteen year ago I came to this Eastern Shore to find my freedom from an island where hypocrisy ruled and integrity was increasingly abandoned and unknown. This Court, this outpost of that lost island, has today awarded not justice, but a trio of actors and thieves who would suppose to act a play about a mortal nation on God's holy day. Well I say no man living has the right to pen one twist in the mysterious plot God Himself has written for this new world. God has cast the parts. God has directed the action. His son has the leading role. And it is for no actor, thief, Reverend or Judge to explain any scene or act. The Revelation will be had within. Christ will come again, but only inside the hearts of those not shut up in unbelief.

This has been eliciting increasing shock and outrage from the CROWD, and music has already crept back in, growing.

EDWARD MARTIN   So howl ye proud Preachers, the Lord is coming! Thy false Kingdom will be taken from thee! / Repent, and give over deceiving human kind! Thou hath shut the kingdom of heaven against men to the destruction of thousands and ten thousands who have perished under thy ways!

EDMOND PORE   Mister Martin... Mister Martin, you will stand down! ...I will not have this blasphemy in this Court! ...Mister Martin you will be silent!

And now EDWARD MARTIN is just that. The music too.

EDMOND PORE   Sheriff Fawsett: take this man out! This Court is adjourned!

EDWARD MARTIN is taken out by JOHN FAWSETT and the crowd goes wild against him while he shouts:

EDWARD MARTIN This is not over! This is not over!

Then the CROWD applaud, gathering around the defendants and the bar for a drink. TRYAL PORE sings again. Eventually EVERYONE else exits. DANIEL PRICHARD catches TRYAL PORE'S eye on the way out, and she meets it, which does not go unnoticed by WILLIAM DARBY.

TRYAL PORE *(sings)*
That's the end Judge Edmond Pore
The stage is dark, there is no more
Justice was decreed! Well done!
Now you can drink your wine and toast that you have won

And off they go, the Accomack Three
The crowd as one raves openly
"Can you believe it, Edward Martin dared
To make a scene against our Judge Pore's decree?"

Now the summer will be autumn
And the waiting is over done
The seasons have changed with ease; now will we?

Then the autumn will turn to winter
And the winter won't wait on spring's word
The seasons change with ease; so should we.

Like the way I made eyes with a man I don't know!
Have I done wrong? Will the Lord forgive me even so?
And how will this next season go?

TRYAL PORE's tone shifts down.

TRYAL PORE *(sings)*
And there is no point in guessing
The plan God has in store
If He's written a script at all
It's a riddle and nothing more

So what is the point in staking
Any claim to any chain
If you're honest and you do no wrong
No good Lord would complain
If that's true then it's up to me
To decide how to change
And if it's true that it's up to me
Will I still wait... or change?

Scene Sixteen

> *In the barn on the Pore property. TRYAL PORE is surprised by the arrival of WILLIAM DARBY.*

TRYAL PORE Oh! I didn't notice you there. Is it time for my reading lesson? It has been so long, I've forgotten the hour.

WILLIAM DARBY It was always at this hour. You never forgot.

TRYAL PORE I did not forget. I was thinking is all.

WILLIAM DARBY Practical thoughts?

TRYAL PORE Practical thoughts?

WILLIAM DARBY I've missed our lessons.

TRYAL PORE I have as well.

WILLIAM DARBY I understand why your father felt it unwise that his daughter remain under the tutelage of a possible blasphemer and seditious criminal. And the trials HAVE kept me occupied.

TRYAL PORE I was there every time. I knew you would not be charged in the end. Everyone knew it. It has been all the talk. You still have your popularity.

WILLIAM DARBY What were you thinking so hard on when I startled you just now?

TRYAL PORE I was only thinking.

WILLIAM DARBY On the carpenter Daniel Prichard?

TRYAL PORE Why would I be thinking on the carpenter Daniel Prichard?

WILLIAM DARBY We could have seen each other still. Each time the crowd dispersed from the tavern I could not catch your eye. You were always looking otherwise.

TRYAL PORE You were so taken up by everything – your rehearsals, everyone buying your beer, wanting to talk justice with you. You were even more popular than before and all eyes were on you. I didn't want to draw any attention to us.

WILLIAM DARBY YOU didn't?

TRYAL PORE Wh–! Is it not what you have always advised? That our love remain in secret until it's more – honestly, I don't know what; convenient for you?

WILLIAM DARBY Has Daniel Prichard been courting you? And have you allowed it?

TRYAL PORE He wishes to be seen beside me, in the Church, and for my parents to know of his intentions. I know where HE stands with regard to me.

WILLIAM DARBY Do you know him otherwise?

TRYAL PORE I hear he's very practical. And I imagine he's very dependable.

Anyway he does not seem at all ashamed of what he claims to feel for me.
WILLIAM DARBY I am not ashamed.
TRYAL PORE And I am weary, William Darby, of waiting for you to say as much outside this barn. You have your old life again. You're on everyone's lips. You don't need mine prattling after you. You could have your pick of the girls now, I'm sure. Perhaps you might even find the one you deem worthy of loving freely, in the open air – rather than FOR free, without having to compensate her with a promise she can understand.
WILLIAM DARBY You love freedom as much as I. You yearn for independence of body and soul as deeply as I do.
TRYAL PORE Yes! Yes! So take my hand! And I will run with you! ...You stand there. I give myself to you and you stand there. I cannot reconcile the stone that overcomes you when I offer myself. So easy like a breeze I give myself to you; and you hesitate. You say "dangerously fond" and "unashamed" and every word short of "love." For all the words you have taught me to understand you have no idea how even to speak the dearest of them all. And yet you judge and taught me to judge my neighbors for their hypocrisy! For boiling in lust while smiting others who dare give their body up to honesty! For begging God to forgive them while they do not forgive their friends without a sickening spectacle of forced tears and false humility! Your independent mind has not unleashed you anymore than their hypocrisy has freed them! You don't know love! You wouldn't know freedom if it tackled you in this straw–!

WILLIAM DARBY has tackled TRYAL PORE and kisses her madly. TRYAL PORE returns it immediately. But then:

TRYAL PORE I can't only kiss you anymore.
WILLIAM DARBY I won't only kiss you anymore. I will take your hand. I will run with you. Out those doors if you wish it! Into the Church if you ask it! Shouting your name if you desire it! I do love you! I love you! As foolish as I am and have been I–

TRYAL PORE kisses WILLIAM DARBY and they sink to their knees.

Just then, DANIEL PRICHARD enters with some urgency and is surprised by what HE finds.

DANIEL PRICHARD William Darby? William Dar–!

WILLIAM DARBY and TRYAL PORE heard him but failed to disentangle themselves from one another sufficiently before being seen.

DANIEL PRICHARD ...I've been sent by Sheriff Fawsett. Fowkes' Tavern has caught fire and I am to muster every available man.

WILLIAM DARBY Caught fire?

DANIEL PRICHARD They say it is the revenge of Edward Martin. Captain Pore is at the creek untying his skiff. He said I would find you here tutoring his daughter–

TRYAL PORE –Daniel–

DANIEL PRICHARD –and you should travel with him.

WILLIAM DARBY Daniel.

DANIEL PRICHARD You had better go.

...WILLIAM DARBY exits. Then:

TRYAL PORE Daniel.

DANIEL PRICHARD You are a fornicator, Tryal Pore.

TRYAL PORE ...I am not.

DANIEL PRICHARD I saw it there. And if I saw it there just now, God already had. May He forgive you when you repent.

TRYAL PORE I will not repent. I love William Darby.

DANIEL PRICHARD He is an ungodly man, Tryal Pore.

TRYAL PORE He is your friend.

DANIEL PRICHARD He was kind, I thought; I have not had cause to hate him before. But he has never believed in God.

WILLIAM DARBY returns, unseen by DANIEL PRICHARD.

DANIEL PRICHARD I doubt he has spoken one word to God. His soul is lost. To see you kneeling in the dirt with him. He is a fornicator. And you are a fornicator.

WILLIAM DARBY Daniel Prichard. Call me what you like. But you will not slander her name.

DANIEL PRICHARD Your duty is to muster, William Darby, by order of Sheriff Fawsett. Fowkes' Tavern is burning because of you. And Captain Pore who set you free is waiting for you.

WILLIAM DARBY I am truly sorry for Thomas Fowkes and grateful to Captain Pore. But my duty in this moment is to this woman so long as you are blackening her name.

DANIEL PRICHARD Her name was blackened long before I stained my tongue with it.

WILLIAM DARBY Daniel, Tryal Pore is not stained. I love her. You tell that to God.

DANIEL PRICHARD Had I ever lent the Devil my ear as you both have done he might have told me what God, faithful to you in vain, did not. But I was innocent of your true hearts. Now it is my regret. I regret you, Tryal Pore. And I regret, George Derby Junior, having ever looked past your sinful ways. You came to this New World on a pretense and I've kept your secret for you until now. You swayed me with your false charms as you then swayed her, and as she your good student then swayed me too. I will not be swayed longer. God save you both.

>   *DANIEL PRICHARD exits. Music.*

TRYAL PORE What do we do? He will surely accuse us to the congregation.
WILLIAM DARBY And though they will forgive a play when it shares their politics, they will never forgive anyone who enjoys the carnality they deny themselves.
TRYAL PORE We will be hanged! We will be hanged!
WILLIAM DARBY We will not be hanged.
TRYAL PORE How?
WILLIAM DARBY We will go.
TRYAL PORE Where?
WILLIAM DARBY West. Into the wild land. Into the chaos.

>   *Music shifts.*

TRYAL PORE ...Take my hand.

>   *WILLIAM DARBY does.*

TRYAL PORE Daniel Prichard called us fornicators, William Darby.

>   *WILLIAM DARBY understands.*

WILLIAM DARBY He is wrong. We are not fornicators yet.
TRYAL PORE William.
WILLIAM DARBY What have we now to lose?

>   *TRYAL PORE and WILLIAM DARBY stare at one another as they undress hurriedly, and then make love as the flames engulfing Fowkes' Tavern reach up into the night sky.*

Scene Seventeen

>   *Music shifts. WILLIAM DARBY and TRYAL PORE step forward.*

TRYAL PORE *(sings)*
Come and see the view from here
Where the land and sea and the horizon's clear

Still we cannot tell just what is far and near
We must wait until we get there.

Music continues underneath...

WILLIAM DARBY Once upon a time, in the burgeoning town of Pungoteague, Accomack County, neatly nestled on the Eastern Shore of England's – or God's – Colony Virginia, the preceding events took place. What happened next is an epic tale that no summation can do justice – though we try and try, and so shall I.

As WILLIAM DARBY narrates, each of the characters noted steps forward in turn.

WILLIAM DARBY Thomas Fowkes rebuilt his tavern, and his Quakerism continued to be tolerated, despite the laws forbidding it, since he himself continued to supply the local community with what it needed: beer.

Sheriff Fawsett continued to maintain law and order in Pungoteague, all the while endeavoring to keep Cornelius Watkins out of trouble.

Cornelius Watkins failed in every business venture he pursued. Still, his performance as The Bear left him a popular figure in the community, and he was frequently engaged as a witness in the Court, where, as a lobbyist for anyone who hired him, he earned money for his entertaining if not always fully informed testimonies.

Phillip Howard died in a drunken skiff accident.

Edward Martin was arrested for the burning of Fowkes' Tavern and condemned as a Quaker terrorist. His trial lasted only one hour and that same day he was executed on the public scaffold.

Captain Edmond Pore, on the recommendation of Major Howell Cross, was eventually appointed to the Higher Court in Jamestown. He moved there with his wife, Constance Pore, and they remained in Jamestown for the rest of their days.

Daniel Prichard, though he continued to do well on his land and with his expanding carpentry business, did not marry for many years. Following his failed courtship of Tryal Pore, which indeed ended with his publicly accusing both she and William Darby of fornication, his practical disposition gradually turned to one of determined perfectionism. When he did eventually marry, he and his wife bore two point five children, and cut down every tree on their property in order to surround the entire four hundred fifty acres with a long white picket fence.

WILLIAM DARBY extends a hand toward TRYAL PORE, who takes it.

WILLIAM DARBY Tryal Pore, and William Darby, confessed to the crime of fornication. With William's recently acquired popularity now ruined by sex scandal, and seeing no future together in Pungoteague, late one moonlit night they escaped and ran off together. They earned money where they could as troubadours, singing original songs and performing political monologues. After one such performance in a tavern in Massachusetts, Tryal and William were arrested and condemned as witches for the singing of unholy music. Side by side, they were hanged on the public scaffold and, as was the custom, their bodies then burned. Throughout their hanging, and even as they were consumed by flames, onlookers were amazed to see that each never let go of the other's hand.

TRYAL PORE (*sings*)
Here life comes and now it's gone
Can we ever measure what we've lost and won?
Can a word articulate the setting sun
Or a song the morning after?

Choice can leave us wanting more
Everyday we hope to leap and then to soar
Can we hope to understand the mighty chore
Of this question we call "Freedom?"

Music continues underneath...

WILLIAM DARBY And, as for the colonies, they continued to prosper. The Dutch and the Spanish eventually left, and the British Empire secured the east coast for itself. By 1776, the desire for independence had spread like wildfire across the colonies, which revolted against the British government, and won. The then thirteen colonies were declared the United States, and, over the years, grew to forty-eight, and eventually fifty. A civil war between the northern and southern states resulted in the defeat of the south and a permanent predilection in the Union for only two points of view, political or otherwise. Also, the slaves had been freed, but not really. More years passed, and more immigrants came from more countries. More Indians who had never been to India were turned into alcoholics robbed and/or slaughtered. More land was developed, more cities founded, and ever greater financial gains were reaped. The United States, having already lost its innocence in the Civil War, lost it again in World War One, then again in the Great Depression, a fourth time in World War Two, a fifth in Vietnam, and a sixth on the 11th of September, 2001. But despite its repeated innocence and guilt, successes and failures, heros and villains, and ups and downs, during the first two centuries of its existence and on into the third, the United States continued to surprise, inspire, and perplex the world with its great achievement – an experiment in democracy unequalled, unprecedented, and unrepeatable anywhere in the world, making the young nation a symbol of not just Freedom, but of Freedom's very precariousness, preciousness, difficulty and cost, as well as the place where any hopeful soul might strive to build a new home, for a new life, in a New World. With a well-funded theater playing to packed houses in every community!

> *EVERYONE cheers. TRYAL PORE wraps things up with the celebratory end of her Anthem.*

TRYAL PORE *(sings)*
Tides will rise and empires fall
And a grain of sand can slip and change us all
In the end what will it take to heed the call
Of the heart that knows the anthem?

> *ALL throw their hats in the air and yell:*

ALL Hey!

> *The end.*

Mary Stuart

Adapted from Friedrich Schiller's *Maria Stuart*

Mary Stuart

Mary Stuart was originally commissioned and produced by The Shotgun Players, Berkeley, CA. Patrick Dooley, Artistic Director. Liz Lisle, Managing Director. The world premiere was given there on October 8, 2010. The production was directed by the author, with the following cast and staff:

MARY STUART	Stephanie Gularte
PAULET	Jesse Caldwell
MORTIMER	Ryan Tasker
BURLEIGH	Peter Ruocco
SHREWSBURY	John Mercer
LEICESTER	Scott Coopwood
QUEEN ELIZABETH	Beth Wilmurt
AUBESPINE / DAVISON	Dara Yazdani
Scenery	Nina Ball
Costumes	Christine Crook
Lights	Jacob Petrie & Joan Arhelger
Sound	David Graves
Properties	Megan Lush
Stage Manager	Erin J. Searfus

Characters

> *Mary Stuart*
> *Paulet*
> *Mortimer*
> *Burleigh*
> *Shrewsbury*
> *Leicester*
> *Queen Elizabeth*
> *Aubespine*
> *Davison*

Note

> *A slash in the dialogue (/) indicates that the next actor should start their*

line, creating overlapping speech.

Act One
Scene One

> *An interrogation room. Enter MARY, MORTIMER and PAULET. MORTIMER seats MARY roughly in a chair, then exits.*

PAULET Where did the ring come from? Wherever it was, no doubt there are more. And letters written in French, the language of England's enemy. With time on hand an evil mind keeps busy. Your contemplations would incite hope and prompt daring.

MARY "A noble heart in time resigns itself to life's calamities; And yet it cuts one to the soul to part with all life's little outward niceties."

PAULET For a lewd and vicious life, privation and humbling are suitable penance. And still you have found the means to stretch your arm out into the world from these bonds and inflame this country with the torch of civil war. Our scaffold bends beneath the weight of daily use, and we'll never see the end of it until you yourself break it with your neck.

MARY Since that day I set foot in this country, and as a fugitive, a suppliant, came begging for protection, I have been condemned despite the law of Nations.

PAULET Despite the law of Nations? You came to us a murderess, from a throne which you repeatedly disgraced, chased from it by your own people! A hellish duty that's been intrusted to me, to guard this cunning disaster! Every night I lie awake in fear that morning will give rise to a new light that confirms my apprehensions. At least now there is some hope that all my fears will soon come to an end.

MARY Paulet. You have confiscated what I myself hoped to deliver to you today – a letter for my royal sister of England. Give me your word, sir, that you will deliver it to her directly and not into Burleigh's false hands.

PAULET I will consider what is best to do.

MARY Paulet. In this letter I ask of her a favor, that she herself will meet with me in person. I was brought before a court of men. It is to her only, a sister, a queen, a woman, that I can open myself.

PAULET You have often entrusted your fate and honor to men far less worthy of your respect than these.

MARY And I ask of you another favor. For too long in this prison I have missed the Church's comfort.

PAULET Whenever you wish it, the dean shall come to see you.

MARY *(sharply)* I want nothing from your dean! I demand a priest from my own church!

PAULET moves to go.

MARY You go, Sir? Without relieving the uncertainty that beats my fearful, anxious heart? I am shut off from the world. No voice can reach me. No word. A month has passed already since they surprised me, forced me, unprepared, without an advocate, to stand before their unprecedented court. Then like ghosts they came, and then vanished, and since that day all mouths are shut to me and I wait here in silence. Break this. Let me know what I still have to fear, and what to hope for.

PAULET Close your account with heaven.

MARY Then is my case closed?

PAULET I do not know.

MARY Am I condemned?

PAULET I do not know, my Lady.

MARY People love to go to work quickly here. Is it intended that my murderer shall surprise me, like the judges?

PAULET England's sovereigns need fear nothing but their conscience and their parliament. What justice has decreed, her fearless hand will execute openly and for the world to see.

Exit PAULET.

Scene Two

MARY alone.

MARY Today is the anniversary of that unhappy day. Once again. Fresh blood rises up from the shallow grave of that long since forgiven crime. Others committed it. But I knew it. And I allowed it. I lured my husband with flatteries into death's embrace. And dragged that heavy guilt over my young life. I was provoked by bloody injuries and by the rude presumptions of that man, whom my love raised up above all others. Through my bridal chamber I led him to my throne. Could he forget that his golden life was the child of my generous love? He did. Forget. He, my wealth's creature, wished to play my king. He abused me with his brutal manners, suspected and defied me. Before my very eyes he had my beautiful singer, my Rizio, murdered. All I did was avenge with blood a bloody deed. And blood, I think, will soon take its revenge on me. I was not myself when I consented to my crime. The madness of a desperate love possessed me. I belonged to that seducer, Bothwell, who ruled me with his shameful, overbearing will, stirred my affections with his flatteries, hatched the plot against my husband in hopes that, having already usurped him in my bed, he might take his place beside my throne as well. Which I helped him do. Yet I am not so lost. And whatever cause I may have for penitence, I am not guilty in England. Not England's queen, not England's parliament is my judge. Here it is only Might that oppresses me. While I must make my peace with myself.

Scene Three

Enter MORTIMER.

MORTIMER Don't be afraid, my Lady. Learn here who I am.

MORTIMER hands MARY a letter.

MARY "Confide in Mortimer, who brings you this. You have no truer friend in England." From my uncle, the Cardinal of Lorraine, in France.

MORTIMER Pardon me, my Queen, for the hateful mask which has cost me so much pain to wear till now. I was twenty years old, raised strictly and with discipline to hate the papacy, when an irresistible desire for foreign lands took hold of me. I resolved to leave this country and its puritanical faith far, far behind me. It was the time of the great jubilee and crowds of palmers filled the streets. It was as if all humankind were wandering in pilgrimage toward the heavenly kingdom. The tide of believers carried me, surged me onward and poured me into the streets of Rome. I had never felt the power of art till then. The church that raised me hates the senses and their charms. It tolerates no beautiful image, adoring only the unseen, cerebral world. Imagine my feelings then as I approached the threshold of the Roman churches and heard their heavenly music floating in the air where the Highest, the Most Glorious pervaded.

MARY Spare me this hopeful picture of life you paint for me. I am a prisoner.

MORTIMER I was a prisoner too, my Queen. But my prison gates flew open when my spirit felt its liberty. I met the Cardinal of Guise. He showed me how the glinting light of reason only leads us to eternal error, that what the heart is called on to believe the eye must see.

MARY Then you are one of the many thousands whom he has led to salvation.

MORTIMER Yes. Yes. ...One day I was wandering through the bishop's home, and I was struck by a fine portrait of a woman. The bishop said to me, "You would do well to linger in deep emotion near this lovely face. For the most beautiful of womankind is also unmatched in her calamity. She is a prisoner for our holy faith." When I then learned you had been taken from Lord Shrewsbury's charge and into the arms of my uncle's care, it struck me, I knew that the wondrous hand of heaven was stretching out to me. Fate had cried out my name and chosen Me to rescue You. ...You have been deprived here of all life's graces, and yet all around you there is life and eternal light. ...But I come with dreadful news.

MARY Is it my sentence?

MORTIMER The judges have given the verdict "guilty," and the Parliament has eagerly and urgently demanded its execution. Only Queen Elizabeth delays it, but craftily, rather than from any feeling of humanity or of mercy, so that she may be forced to yield.

MARY I've prepared myself for this. After all the cruelty I have suffered I can understand how they now dare not restore my liberty. I know what they mean to do. But for shame she cannot dare lay my crowned head on the executioner block.

MORTIMER She would dare it.

MARY She doesn't fear the revenge of France?

MORTIMER She is locking up an everlasting peace with France. The Duke from Anjou offers her his hand and his throne.

MARY Will the king of Spain not take up arms?

MORTIMER She doesn't fear a world of arms so long as she remains at peace with her people.

MARY ...It's not the scaffold I fear. There are many other quieter means. Before an executioner is found for me, they'll let a murderer do his work.

MORTIMER Neither openly nor in disguise shall any murderer take your life. Twelve friends are allied with me, and pledged early today upon the sacrament to free you from this place by force.

MARY No, no no, not by force! My enemies are watchful and the power is in their hands. The free will of Elizabeth alone can open them to me.

MORTIMER Never hope for that.

MARY "Never hope for that."

MORTIMER Never hope for that!

MARY There is one man alive that can open her. Leicester.

MORTIMER ...Leicester?

MARY Yes.

MORTIMER The favorite of Elizabeth, your bloodiest enemy. Leicester.

MARY If I am to be saved it is by him alone.

MORTIMER My Queen. This is a mystery–.

MARY Leicester will solve this mystery. Give me something to write with.

> *MORTIMER gives MARY a pen and paper. MARY writes a note and gives it back to MORTIMER.*

MARY Go to Leicester. Confide in him.

MORTIMER My Queen.

MORTIMER exits.

Scene Four

Enter BURLEIGH and PAULET.

PAULET You wished today to know your fate. Lord Burleigh brings it to you now. Bear it with humility.

BURLEIGH I come as an envoy from the court.

MARY Lord Burleigh lends his mouth to the court, to which he has already lent his spirit.

BURLEIGH You have to the court submitted–

MARY –Submitted? Submitted? I ha–! I have in no way: submitted!

BURLEIGH You heard the points of accusation and answered to them before the court.

MARY I was through deceptive cunning, and with the confidence of my good cause and strong defence, persuaded to listen to the points of accusation and prove their falsity. This I did; out of personal respect for the Lords, not for their office, which I reject.

BURLEIGH Whether or not you acknowledge the court is only a formality which cannot stop the course of justice. You breathe England's air, enjoy the protections and benefits of its laws, and so you are also subject to its rule.

MARY I breathe the air of an English prison! I am not this country's citizen! ...I am the free Queen of a foreign land.

BURLEIGH And think that bloody discord in foreign lands will go unpunished. Where would the state's security stand if justice could not as freely strike the guilty head of an imperial foreigner as it would a beggar's?

MARY I do not claim exemption from justice. It is this court of judges I reject.

BURLEIGH They are the foremost men of this country, too independent to be anything else but honest, afraid of neither kings nor bribery. They are men whose names I need but mention to dispel any doubt, any suspicion, that one might raise against them.

MARY I am astonished to hear such control from that mouth that always brings me disaster. How can I, an unlearned woman, compete with so artful a speaker. Yes, very well! Were these Lords as you described them then I must be silent, my cause hopelessly lost were they to pronounce me guilty. Yet these names, which you would be so pleased to name, the weight of which should crush me, I see playing an entirely different role in this country's history. I see these high Nobles of England, this Empire's magisterial Senate, like slaves in a harem flattering the Sultan moods of my great uncle, Henry the Eighth. I see this noble House of Lords make laws and destroy them, bind marriages and dissolve them, and, as the Almighty commandeth, disinherit England's first daughters and brand them with the name of bastards today, then tomorrow crown them as queens. I see these worthy Peers with their nimble conscience under four reigns change their beliefs four times!

BURLEIGH You say you are a foreigner to England's laws. In England's misfortunes you are well versed.

MARY It is said your intentions are for the good of this country, that you are incorruptible, vigilant, that not your own benefit but the advantage of your sovereigns and your country alone rules you. You should question yourself, then, that you do not mistake the benefit of the state for justice. It is an ancient saying that the English cannot be just with the Scots. Therefor it is tradition that before a court neither an Englishman against a Scot, nor a Scot against an Englishman, may testify. Dire necessity made this peculiar law. Nature threw these two fiery nations into the ocean on the same plank, divided it unequally, and bade them fight for it. Hand on the sword, they've watched each other threateningly – for a thousand years, Burleigh! No enemy pesters England that the Scots do not join to help. No civil war inflames the cities of Scotland that the English do not fan its fire. This hate will never burn out until finally one scepter reigns across the entire island.

BURLEIGH And a Stuart should grant this happiness to the empire?

MARY Yes. I confess it. I do hold the hope that I will unite these two noble nations under the olive branch, in freedom and in happiness. I didn't believe I'd become the victim of their national hate.

BURLEIGH It was a terrible route you took toward this goal, to set this country on fire and through the flames of civil war strive to mount its throne.

MARY When did I strive for that? Where is the proof?

BURLEIGH It is known that you broke the Law enacted last year, which states, "If a plot henceforth should rise in England, in the name or for the benefit of any claimant to England's crown, justice shall be done on such pretender,

MARY / I–, yes...

BURLEIGH and the guilty party prosecuted unto death." And since it has been proven–

MARY –My Lord Burleigh, I do not doubt that this law, made explicitly for me, written to ruin me, would be used against me.

BURLEIGH You conspired with Babington and his murderous companions to assassinate the Queen of England. You had knowledge of everything they did and from your prison directed the deeply laid plans of your plot.

MARY When?! Paulet: when did I do that? When? Show me the evidence!

BURLEIGH You have already seen the documents, when they were presented to you before the court.

MARY Copies! Written in someone else's hand!

BURLEIGH Babington confessed, before his death, that they were in fact the same documents that he had received from you.

MARY Before his death and wh– Why when he was living was he not brought before me. Why was he then executed so quickly?

BURLEIGH And your house servant confirmed on oath that these were the letters which he had transcribed from your mouth.

MARY And on the testimony of my house servant I am condemned here?

BURLEIGH You yourself confirmed that your house servant is a man of virtue and conscience.

MARY Yes, I knew him to be just that, but a man's virtue is tested under threat. Torture could have frightened him to confess what he would not.

BURLEIGH ...We do not torture. Nobody here was tortured... He swore a free oath.

MARY Good. Good. Stand him before me and let him repeat his testimony to me. I know from Shrewsbury that under this government a statute has been passed that the plaintiff must stand before the defendant. True? Or have I heard falsely? Sir Paulet, I have known you to be an honest man; now prove it to me. Is there no such law in England?

PAULET There is, my Lady. That is the law, it is true.

MARY Burleigh. If I am to be treated so strictly by the laws of England, why was Babington not brought before me, as the law commands? Why not my house servant, who is still alive?

BURLEIGH Don't get yourself worked up, my Lady. Your plot with Babington is not the only–

MARY –It is the only thing that exposes me to the sword of the law. Stay with the point. Don't avoid it.

BURLEIGH It is known that you have corresponded with Mendoza, the ambassador of Spain–

MARY –Stay with the point, Burleigh!

BURLEIGH *(incensed:)* That you have made attempts to topple the religion of this nation, that you have provoked all the kings of Europe to war with England–!

> *BURLEIGH moves suddenly to MARY as if to do fatal violence to her, startling her. PAULET takes a step forward. BURLEIGH stops and then collects himself, as does MARY.*

MARY ...I have done no such things. And yet now I wish I had done such things. ...My Lord Burleigh, I am kept here in prison against all laws of Nations. I did not come to England with a sword in hand. I came as a suppliant, and claimed the sacred rights of hospitality. But Power seized me and prepared chains for me where I'd hoped to find protection. Is my conscience, then, chained to this country? Do I owe a duty? To this country?! If I war with these bonds, it is a sacred right I derive from sad necessity, and whatever in this rightful war is necessary, it is my just right to do. But murder would dishonor me, and I will not stain my hands with it! ...Though she can murder me, she cannot judge me. Let her give up trying to unite the fruits of crime and virtue. And let her dare to shine as what she is. ...Thank you, sir.

Exit BURLEIGH, then PAULET.

Scene Five

Outside the interrogation room. BURLEIGH and PAULET.

BURLEIGH She defies us. She will defy us, even on the steps of the scaffold. This proud heart will not be broken. This condemned Mary Stuart must disappear, quickly.

PAULET This defiance would quickly disappear if one were to take away the excuse for it. If I may say it, irregularities have been allowed in these proceedings. England's enemies will fill the world with spiteful rumors.

BURLEIGH This is what troubles our Queen, that the cause of this disaster, this condemned Mary Stuart, did not die before she set her foot on English soil.

PAULET This country would have been spared a great deal of misfortune.

BURLEIGH Yes, yes. A great deal of misfortune.

PAULET And? ...So?

BURLEIGH And so what? ...She must not live, this Mary Stuart.

BURLEIGH exits, followed by PAULET.

Act Two
Scene One

A conference room. BURLEIGH, LEICESTER, SHREWSBURY, and ELIZABETH.

BURLEIGH One concern! Only one concern occupies this nation! It is a sacrifice that every voice calls for! They demand the head of the Stuart! If you wish to secure the freedom and the truth you have so dearly won, then she must die! If we are not to continue living in fear for your life, then your enemy must be destroyed! We know that not all of our citizens think alike, that Roman idolatry still has many secret admirers on this island who harbor hostile convictions. They have sworn a grim war of extermination against you! No peace can be made with her or with her faction! You must resolve to strike, or suffer! Her life is your death, her death your life!

ELIZABETH My Lord Burleigh, I know the purity that drives your zeal. Yet this wisdom that calls for blood I hate in my deepest soul. Lord Shrewsbury.

BURLEIGH It / is their hatred–!

ELIZABETH –Lord Shrewsbury!

SHREWSBURY To execute the Stuart is an unjust action. You cannot pronounce a sentence upon someone who is not your subject.

ELIZABETH So my council and my Parliament have erred.

BURLEIGH The council and the Parliament have not erred!

SHREWSBURY A majority vote is not proof of justice. England is not the world. Your Parliament is not the association of the human race. Do not say that you must act out of necessity, in urgent obeyance of the people. Your will is free at every moment. Make it known that you detest violence. Show those who wish to counsel you otherwise that you are not pretending, that you are the Queen. You yourself must pass the judgement, you alone!

ELIZABETH Lord Shrewsbury is a friendly advocate for my and England's enemy. I prefer those counsellors who champion my welfare.

Enter PAULET.

PAULET Your Majesty.

ELIZABETH Yes.

PAULET Ambassador Aubespine is here.

ELIZABETH Thank you.

EVERYONE repositions themselves for the arrival of the visitor. PAULET exits and returns with AUBESPINE.

AUBESPINE Your Majesty.

ELIZABETH Monsieur Aubespine. I must tell you again that I am afraid now is not the time to rekindle the subject of joyful marriage. Heaven has cast black and heavy clouds over my country.

AUBESPINE I understand. We only ask your Majesty to promise her royal hand now, and, when happier days come, then give it.

ELIZABETH Without a doubt, Monsieur Ambassador, a marriage with the Duke of Anjou, a royal son of France, would do me honor.

AUBESPINE It is a beautiful hope. Yet it is only a hope, and my King would like more than just that.

ELIZABETH looks at AUBESPINE steadily for a moment, then at the various rings on her fingers. She selects one and removes it.

ELIZABETH This is not yet a chain. But from it a link may grow to bind me.

ELIZABETH passes the ring to AUBESPINE.

ELIZABETH Let it ease any suspicion between our nations.

AUBESPINE This is a day of joy. Would that it could be for all, and that no mourner on this island had cause to weep. The unhappy Princess Mary, who concerns France and Britain alike–

ELIZABETH –Let us not mix two entirely incompatible matters of business. If France is serious in its desire for my accord, it must also share my concerns, and not be friends with my enemies.

AUBESPINE Please. Would it not seem unworthy in your own eyes if in this treaty France forgot this unfortunate woman? Faith and the honor of humanity alone require–

ELIZABETH –By this sentiment I know how to estimate the worth of your intercession, Ambassador Aubespine. Deliver my link.

ELIZABETH indicates to AUBESPINE that he may go.

AUBESPINE Your Majesty.

AUBESPINE exits with PAULET.

SHREWSBURY Burleigh.

BURLEIGH We must / now at once–

SHREWSBURY Burleigh! Burleigh, we want to be the rule of law, not the question of it! We gave her no lawyer!

BURLEIGH Because we needed / an answer–

SHREWSBURY Nobody dares to speak in her favor for fear of meeting your anger. Everything has conspired against her. *(to ELIZABETH:)* You have never seen her face, and nothing in your heart speaks for this stranger. They say, it was she who planned her husband's murder. It's true that she married the murderer. A grievous crime, / without a doubt.

BURLEIGH A / grievous crime–!

ELIZABETH Let him speak.

SHREWSBURY But: it happened in a terrible, unfortunate time, a dreadful civil war. She was completely vulnerable, and sought protection in a powerful man. To you misfortune was a strict school.

ELIZABETH Pardon?

SHREWSBURY You could see no throne ahead of you. You saw the grave was gaping for you at your feet. At Woodstock and in London's gloomy Tower, God taught you to understand your duty through suffering. No flatterers sought you there. There, without distractions from the vanity of the world, at an early age you learned introspection and to collect your mind. No God protected Mary Stuart. As a delicate child she was transplanted to France, a courtyard of carelessness and mindless pleasure. There in a festival of perpetual drunkenness she never heard the truth from any serious voice. Her misfortune was the vain possession of a face that outshone all others in beauty and noble / birth.

ELIZABETH My Lord Shrewsbury. Collect yourself. Leicester, you are silent.

LEICESTER I am silent out of astonishment, my Queen, that they fill your heart with such terrible conceptions, that these fairy tales, which in the streets terrorize the gullible people, should reach the enlightened circle of your council–

BURLEIGH –Fairy tales, all fairy tales, yes?

LEICESTER I am surprised, I will admit, that this country-less Queen from Scotland, who could not manage her small throne, whose own people ridiculed her and exiled her from her country, should as a prisoner become your terror. What, in heaven's name, makes her so terrifying to you? That she makes a claim to this empire?

BURLEIGH Lord Leicester has not always taken this perspective.

LEICESTER It's true, I have given my voice in court to her death.

BURLEIGH To her death?

LEICESTER In the court! Here in council I'll speak otherwise. Is now the time to fear her power, when France, her only protection, has abandoned her? Why, then, rush to her death? She is dead! Contempt is her true death. Let her death sentence stand. And let her live. But with her head forever beneath the axe.

ELIZABETH I have now heard your opinions. This meeting is finished.

Scene Two

Enter PAULET and MORTIMER.

PAULET Your Majesty?

ELIZABETH Yes.

PAULET My nephew, Mortimer.

ELIZABETH motions for MORTIMER to enter the room, where she looks at him steadfastly.

ELIZABETH I welcome you, Mortimer.

PAULET Secret correspondence intended for the Queen of Scotland has been entrusted to him, which he faithfully handed on to us.

ELIZABETH Hmm. ...Your enemies say that you went to school in France and abjured your faith.

MORTIMER I pretended as much, in great hope of serving you, my Queen.
ELIZABETH Well.

> *PAULET steps forward with a letter.*

PAULET Here also is a letter to you from the Queen of Scotland. She asks that you might grant her the concession of meeting with her in person.
BURLEIGH Sir Paulet, as an abettor to murder, she has forfeited the goodwill of any meeting with the face of royalty. She is condemned. Her head is beneath the axe. That sentence cannot be executed if the Queen meets with her, since a meeting with any royal presence signifies pardon, Sir Paulet.

> *...ELIZABETH takes the letter from PAULET and reads it through. The OTHERS watch and wait. ELIZABETH is quieted by the letter. When she is done:*

ELIZABETH What is humanity. What is the happiness of the earth.
SHREWSBURY Your heart has heard God. Obey this heavenly movement.
BURLEIGH Do not let a commendable human emotion mislead you. Do not rob yourself of the freedom to do what is necessary.
LEICESTER The Queen is wise, she does not need our counsel to make the most dignified choice!
ELIZABETH We will find the means to reconcile what grace demands of us with what necessity imposes. Thank you, gentlemen.

> *ALL begin to exit.*

ELIZABETH Mortimer, a word.

> *ALL exit but MORTIMER.*

Scene Three

> *ELIZABETH measures MORTIMER in silence for a long time before speaking.*

ELIZABETH You have shown a courage and a self-possession well beyond your years. Anyone who has learned the art of deception so early and so well is old before his time. You have acquainted yourself with the enemies of England. They pit their hatred irreconcilably against me. God has protected me until now, but the crown staggers on my head so long as she lives.
MORTIMER She does not live, as soon as you command it.
ELIZABETH I would like to let the law act, and my own hand to be kept clean of blood. The sentence has been pronounced. What do I win? It must be

executed, Mortimer. And I must authorize the execution. I will always bear the hate for it. I must take responsibility for it and cannot save appearances. That is the worst part.

MORTIMER Why worry about hateful appearances when the cause is just, my Queen?

ELIZABETH You don't know the world. What one appears to be, all the world judges. What one is, no one cares. No one will be convinced that I am right. So I must be certain that my part in her death remains forever in doubt. With actions of a double nature there is no protection, except the dark.

MORTIMER *(Questioningly)* Then it would very much be for the best if–

ELIZABETH –Indeed, it would be for the best if. ...Finish it.

MORTIMER I will lend you my hand. Save your name as you can.

ELIZABETH When will I lay my head down to sleep quietly again?

MORTIMER The new moon will end your fears.

ELIZABETH Do not be offended should my gratitude remain in the dark. The closest bonds, the dearest, are those that secrecy makes.

Exit ELIZABETH.

MORTIMER False, deceitful queen! As you do the world, so I will deceive you! Trust my arm only and keep yours back. Give the devout appearance of mercy to the world. In the meantime rest your hope on my murderous help, while we win time for her rescue.

Scene Four

Enter PAULET.

PAULET What did the queen say to you?

MORTIMER ...Nothing.

PAULET Mortimer! You are walking on slippery ground. Do not tempt ambition. You will overspend yourself. Do not injure your conscience.

MORTIMER Uncle, what are your concerns?

PAULET However great the promises the Queen makes to you, do not trust her flatteries. They will disown you if you obey them. Have you obeyed them? ...Have you? ...If you have–

LEICESTER has already entered.

LEICESTER –Sir Paulet, a word with your nephew. The Queen is favorably disposed to him. She would like the Stuart put in his custody, in full trust. She relies on him / to–

PAULET –She relies on him. And I rely on myself, and my two open eyes.

Mortimer.

> *Exit PAULET.*

LEICESTER Do you deserve to be trusted?

MORTIMER I would ask this of you.

LEICESTER You said you wished to speak with me in private.

MORTIMER Assure me first that it is safe to do so.

LEICESTER Who assures me about you? I see that you exhibit two different faces in this court, Sir. One of them must be borrowed. Which one is real?

MORTIMER I have the very same doubts concerning you!

LEICESTER ...Which of us, then, shall open the door to confidence?

MORTIMER Whomever is put in the least danger by doing so.

LEICESTER That would be you, Sir.

MORTIMER No. The word of such a powerful Lord as you can beat me to the ground. I have nothing against your rank and favor.

LEICESTER You are mistaken. One contemptuous testimony can bring me down.

MORTIMER ...If the all-powerful Lord Leicester lets himself step down so low to me, and makes such a confession, then I can think a little more highly of myself, and be the example of generosity.

> *MORTIMER abruptly produces the letter from Mary.*

MORTIMER The Queen of Scotland sends this to you.

LEICESTER What? What? Mary! My God!

> *LEICESTER takes up the letter, kisses and then quickly reads it.*

LEICESTER Do you know the contents of this letter?

MORTIMER I do not.

LEICESTER Surely she told you.

MORTIMER She told me nothing. She said that you would explain this mystery.

LEICESTER Tell me first how you earned her trust.

MORTIMER Leicester, I recently went to Rome and disavowed my faith.

LEICESTER I know about your conversion. Pardon my doubts. Give me your hand. I cannot be too careful here.

MORTIMER What careful steps a great Lord must take in this court.

LEICESTER You are surprised, Sir, that my heart has so quickly turned toward Mary. The compulsion of the times made me her opponent. She was once betrothed to me, you know. My ambition made me indifferent to her youth and beauty. At the time I thought Mary's hand was too small for mine. I hoped to possess the Queen of England. And now after years of tedious courtship, bitter years sacrificed to the gods of Elizabeth's vanity, now I am searching for a plank to grab onto in this unfortunate shipwreck. And my heart turns itself again to this first beautiful hope. Yes. My heart compared, and I felt, what a jewel I lost. With horror I saw her fall into the deepest misery. She fell through my mistakes. Now the hope wakes that I still can save her. And this letter you brought to me assures me that she will forgive me, if I save her.

MORTIMER But you did nothing to save her. You let her be condemned. You gave your own voice to her death. A / miracle must happen!

LEICESTER That has cost me enough agony, Mortimer! But don't think that I would have allowed her to go to her death. I hoped, and still hope, to prevent the worst until a way to free her shows itself.

MORTIMER That has been found. I will free her. That is why I am here. The steps have already been taken, and your assistance assures our success.

LEICESTER What are you saying? How? You would–

MORTIMER I will crack open this prison by force. I have friends in place. Everything is ready.

LEICESTER You have accomplices? What are you pulling me into?

MORTIMER Our plan was made without you. Without you it would have been accomplished, had she not wished to owe her rescue to you.

LEICESTER So, can you assure me with complete certainty that my name has not been mentioned in this plan?

MORTIMER So scrupulous. You want to rescue and possess Mary. You suddenly, unexpectedly find friends. But you show more embarrassment than joy.

LEICESTER There is nothing to be gained with force. It's too dangerous.

MORTIMER Delay is also dangerous.

LEICESTER I tell you, it cannot be risked.

MORTIMER No, not for you, who wants to possess her. We want only to save her and are not concerned with risk.

LEICESTER I see the nets that surround us. If we fail we'll tear her down with us.

MORTIMER If we risk nothing she will never be saved.

LEICESTER You consider nothing, you hear nothing. With fierce, blind impetuousness you will destroy everything that's been so well under way.

MORTIMER What have you done to save her? If I were now idiot enough to murder Mary Stuart as the Queen has ordered I do, tell me what measures you have taken to preserve her life.

LEICESTER Did the Queen give you this order?

MORTIMER She made a mistake in trusting me, as Mary did with you.

LEICESTER And have you promised? Have you?

MORTIMER Naturally, so that she would not solicit another hand I offered mine.

LEICESTER This might give us space. She relies on your bloody service, the death sentence remains unexecuted, and we gain time.

MORTIMER No, we are losing time!

LEICESTER She's counting on you, Mortimer! Maybe I can convince her to see Mary. This will bind her hands. Burleigh is right. By law the sentence cannot be enforced if they meet face to face.

MORTIMER And what do you achieve through this? She will never be free! Even the least that can come of it is eternal prison. A bold action is needed to end this. Why will you not take it? Forget pretending! Act openly!

LEICESTER Do you know this country? Do you know how things stand in this court? Take my advice. Do not do anything rash. Go. Go!

MORTIMER exits.

LEICESTER Mary.

LEICESTER exits.

Scene Five

ELIZABETH'S office. ELIZABETH alone. Enter LEICESTER.

LEICESTER Elizabeth.

ELIZABETH is startled.

ELIZABETH Leicester. What are you doing in here? You look embarrassed.

LEICESTER At the sight of you. Your beauty. At times I stand blinded by it.

LEICESTER sighs.

ELIZABETH What are you sighing about?

LEICESTER Have I no reason to sigh? When I look at you I feel again that unnamed pain of impending loss.

ELIZABETH What do you lose?

LEICESTER Your heart.

ELIZABETH ...Pity me. Don't blame me. I am not to question my heart, which would have chosen otherwise. The Stuart was allowed to let her hand give way as she liked. She allowed herself everything, drank down the entire cup of happiness.

LEICESTER And now she drinks from the bitter cup of suffering.

ELIZABETH She never respected the world's opinion. It was easy for her to live. She never invited the yoke upon her neck that I submitted myself to. I could also have made claims to befriending a life of earth and air. But I preferred strict kingly duties. And yet she won the favor of all men. The young and old alike jostled around her. And is it really true she is so beautiful? ...Why are you looking at me so strangely?

LEICESTER He is of royal blood is he not? The Duke of Anjou is of royal blood; which I am not. Yet despite all whom the world might offer, there is not one living on this round earth who feels more adoration for you than I. The Duke of Anjou has never seen you. He can only love your glory and royal luster. I love you. If you were the poorest farm girl, and I born the greatest prince of the world, I would kneel down to you and... I think of you next to Mary. The shame I do to her, which she deserves to see with her own eyes: how very much the force of your nobility would conquer her.

ELIZABETH Yes, you want to see her.

LEICESTER She asks it as a favor. Grant it to her as a punishment. You dazzled me like a shining light when I came into the room. If you, like now, just as you are, appeared before / her–

ELIZABETH *(laughs)* Like now–? no no!

LEICESTER Yes, also the art of governing justifies that you see her, to win public opinion through an open act of generosity. Afterwards, you may do whatever you like, and be done with the hateful enemy.

ELIZABETH ...If I do something foolish, Leicester, it is your fault, not mine.

Act Three
Scene One

An outdoor garden area. MARY enters. PAULET is with her.

MARY Let me enjoy this new freedom. Let me be a child, test my weightless steps on the green carpet of the meadows. I want to dream freely and happily. Does the sky's wide heavenly womb not surround me? My eyes, free and untethered, indulge themselves in unmeasured space. The clouds that chase the afternoon, they search for the distant ocean of France. Rushing clouds. Sailors of the sky. Whoever wanders with you, sails with you. Give a friendly salute to my childhood land. *(to PAULET)* You want to gradually widen my prison, through small steps acclimate me to larger steps, until finally I look at the face of that gang who unties me forever?

PAULET Have I finally done well? Do I for once deserve your thanks?

MARY How so? Is it you who grants this favor to me? You did it?

PAULET Why should it not be me? I went to Queen Elizabeth and gave her your letter.

MARY Really? You did it? You brought it to her? And this freedom I now enjoy is the fruit of this letter.

PAULET And not the only. Prepare yourself for a greater reward still.

MARY For a greater. What do you mean by that?

PAULET In a few moments she will stand before you.

MARY Who? Elizabeth?

PAULET Yes. ...Is it now not right? Was it not your wish? It was granted to you earlier than you thought. You have always been such a quick tongue, now stick to your words, now is the moment to speak.

MARY Paulet. Why did you not prepare me for this? Now I am not ready, not now! What was the highest favor I could obtain is now terrible for me!

Enter SHREWSBURY.

SHREWSBURY Collect yourself! This is the decisive hour.

MARY I have prepared myself for so long. Now there is nothing in me, nothing in this moment.

SHREWSBURY However great your inner struggle, obey the time and the law of the hour. She has the power, be humble.

MARY No! Never!

SHREWSBURY Do it now!

MARY She has insulted me too greatly! There can never be reconciliation between us!

SHREWSBURY Forget everything! Think only how you will receive her submissively. ...Please.

MARY ...Is Burleigh also with her?

SHREWSBURY No one is with her but Count Leicester.

MARY Leicester?

SHREWSBURY It is by his work that the Queen granted a meeting with you.

Enter LEICESTER. Then enter ELIZABETH. At some point MORTIMER enters, not hiding but unobtrusively and unnoticed.

ELIZABETH Who is the lady?

Awkward silence.

MARY My god. No heart speaks from this face.

LEICESTER It has happened, my Queen. And now let the Heavens lead your steps higher, and allow generosity and compassion.

SHREWSBURY Let yourself be favorable. Let your eyes judge this unfortunate person who stands before you.

MARY I will forget who I am, and what I suffered. I will lay myself out before her, she who pushed me down to this disgrace. ...Heaven has sided with you, sister.

ELIZABETH You are where you should be, Lady Stuart.

MARY My fortune, my life, my everything hangs on the strength of my words to loosen my heart that I may set yours free.

ELIZABETH What do you have to say to me?

MARY I cannot speak for myself without accusing you severely, and I do not want to do that. The way you have dealt with me is not right. I am a queen. Like you. I came to you like a suppliant. And you mocked me with the sacred laws of hospitality, locking me in a prison. You stood me before a disgraceful court. But I will blame everything on fate.

ELIZABETH Not fate. Your own black heart is to blame.

MARY No. No. You are not guilty. I am also not guilty. An evil spirit rose out from the abyss to ignite the hate in our hearts. We grew up with it, and bad people fanned the fatal flames with their breath. That is the curse of Kings, that when they are divided they tear the world into hatred. But now there is no other mouth between us. Name my fault. I will fully satisfy you.

ELIZABETH Nothing hostile had happened between us, when your uncle announced to me the feud. Who did he not call against me? Even here in the free place of my own country, he blew the flames of outrage at me with the tongues of priests and the people's swords, terrible weapons of pious insanity. But God is with me. The blow was aimed at my head, and for that yours falls–.

MARY –No, no. You will not use your power so bloodily.

ELIZABETH Who shall stop me? I only practice what your priests teach. Saint Bartholomew schooled me.

MARY Sister, name my fault to me.

ELIZABETH ...What assurance can be granted to me should I magnanimously loosen your bonds? Force is now the only security. There can be no alliance with a coalition of snakes.

MARY You have only ever regarded me as an enemy and a stranger.

ELIZABETH Your friendship is abroad, Lady Stuart. The papacy, the monk is your brother. That you might still seduce my people in my lifetime, that all might turn to the new rising sun / and–

MARY Rule in peace! I abdicate any claim to this kingdom. Not for all the riches of this land, not for all the countries that the sea embraces, would I like to stand in your place as you stand before me now.

ELIZABETH You confess at last that you are conquered?

MARY Yes. Yes. You have achieved it. I am now but the shadow of Mary. You have done your worst to me. Make an end. Say it. Say it to me. Say to me, "You are free, Mary. You have felt my power, now learn to worship my generosity." Say it, and I will take my life and my freedom as a gift from your hands.

ELIZABETH ...Have all your plots run out? Are there no more murderers on the way? ...Yes, it is over, Lady Stuart. The world has other concerns.

MARY Sister. Sist– ...I have endured what a human being can endure. ...The throne of England is desecrated by a bastard! The British people are cheated by a cunning juggler! Woe to you that day the world draws the robe of honor from your deeds and unveils the raging hypocrisy that's blackened your heart! My sins were human, the fault of youth! I never denied or hid them! I made no false appearances! The worst of me is known and I am better than the fame I bear for it! If justice ruled, you now would lie before me in the dust! For I am your King!

Exit ALL but MARY and MORTIMER.

MORTIMER You have won. You were the Queen, she the criminal.

MARY Did you speak with Leicester, deliver to him my letter?

MORTIMER Hope nothing from him. Despise him and forget him!

MARY What? Then it's over?

MORTIMER The coward loves his life. Whoever will save you and call you his must be able to boldly embrace death.

MARY He will do nothing for me?

MORTIMER Don't deceive yourself anymore. Just as the Queen left you now, just as this meeting went, so is everything lost, every means to mercy gone. Action is needed now! Daring must decide! To win everything, everything must be risked! You must be free before the morning comes!

MARY And– How is that possible?

MORTIMER I have gathered the Fellowship. A priest took our confession and for every sin gave us absolution, absolved also every crime we will commit! We received the final sacrament and are ready for the final journey!

MARY Oh God, what terrible preparation!

MORTIMER Every sin has already been forgiven. I can do the worst, and I will do it. I will also murder the Queen. I have sworn it on the Host. I will save you. If it costs a thousand lives, I will save you, I will do it, yes, as God lives, I swear it. I will also possess you.

MARY Oh. Possess. Possess? Was I born only to awaken frenzy? Have hate and love sworn to terrorize me?

Gunshots are heard from elsewhere.

MORTIMER Yes, as fervently as they hate you I love you! They want to behead you, this neck, to cut through this dazzling white with a hatchet! Offer to the living god of joy what you must sacrifice to bloody hate! Inspire your happy lover with these charms that are no longer yours! These beautiful locks of hair are forfeited to the dark forces of death; use them to entwine your slave forever! Why do the brave shed their blood? Is Life not the highest good of Life? You are not unfeeling. The world does not accuse you of cold severity. Love's hot prayer can stir you.

MARY You're insane.

Enter PAULET and SHREWSBURY.

PAULET Here is the murderess. Come, come. My Lady, come back with us to the prison.

SHREWSBURY Please.

Exit SHREWSBURY with MARY.

PAULET The Queen of England. She has been murdered. Mortimer.

Exit PAULET.

MORTIMER The Queen is murdered! No. No, no no, I only dreamed it. A mad fever presses to my senses as true and real what I'd only done in my horrible thoughts. She is murdered! She is down! And Mary will rise to the throne of England!

Exit MORTIMER.

Act Four
Scene One

The conference room. BURLEIGH and LEICESTER.

BURLEIGH Now, my Lord from Leicester, how is the Queen?

LEICESTER She lives, my Lord from Burleigh.

BURLEIGH Good.

LEICESTER Yes, good.

BURLEIGH I understand it was not done by the British people. It was a Frenchman.

LEICESTER It was a papist, Lord Burleigh.

BURLEIGH This means England will not marry with France.

LEICESTER And so you loosen again the alliance that you so busily worked to tie up. You have earned little thanks from England, you could have spared yourself the trouble.

BURLEIGH My purpose was good. Was right. God directed it otherwise. Anyone with so clean a conscience is doing well.

LEICESTER Well. The mysterious means of Burleigh are well known, when he is on the hunt for treason. Now is a good time for you. Now a court of inquisitions will be opened. All of England lies on your shoulders.

BURLEIGH You were the one who, behind my back, wished to lure the Queen to the Stuart, or?

LEICESTER Behind your back! When have I been shy to act in front of your face?

BURLEIGH You did not lead the Queen to the Stuart. It was the Queen who so graciously led you there. Is that not how it was?

LEICESTER What do you mean by that, sir?

BURLEIGH This is the generosity and graciousness that so suddenly came to you in council: that the Stuart is so pathetic, so weak an enemy that it would hardly be worth our trouble to stain ourselves with her blood. A fine plan! Finely sharpened! What a pity, terrible pity, to have sharpened it so finely that your point broke! Pity, pity!

LEICESTER Say that to me before the Queen!

BURLEIGH Very gladly. Meet me there. And see to it that there your eloquence does not fail you.

Exit BURLEIGH.

LEICESTER I've been discovered! I've been seen through! God, if he has evidence, what should I do? Oh God!

Enter MORTIMER.

MORTIMER Leicester, are we alone?

LEICESTER What are you doing here now? What do you want?

MORTIMER They're on our heels, on yours too. They know that secret meetings have been held with the French Ambassador, Aubespine.

LEICESTER What concern is that to me?

MORTIMER That the murderer would be found here as well!

LEICESTER That is your affair. What bloody outrage have you started that you've now tangled me up in?

MORTIMER Listen to me.

LEICESTER Go to hell!

MORTIMER You don't want to listen me. I have come to warn you that you have also been found out.

LEICESTER What?

MORTIMER Mary Stuart's room was searched through and they found there

LEICESTER / No.

MORTIMER a letter she had just addressed to you in which she calls on you to keep your word.

LEICESTER No!

MORTIMER Lord Burleigh has the letter.

LEICESTER Burleigh has the letter? Oh god. I'm lost! Oh my God!

MORTIMER Seize the moment. Go to him. Save yourself. Save her. Swear from now on to do what you must to avoid the worst. I can't do anything more here. My allies have scattered. Our fellowship is blown apart. I will hurry to Scotland to gather new friends. It's now on you to do what you can, what a bold face must.

LEICESTER Yes, Mortimer, yes yes. I will do it. Help! Treason! Traitor! The conspiracy is found out! Take this traitor into custody and guard him well! I will bring the message to the Queen myself! I am sorry Mortimer.

Exit LEICESTER.

MORTIMER Yes, I deserve this. Who told me to trust this wretched man? He steps on my neck, and builds a bridge to safety over my downfall! But I am free. And in this last moment my heart shall freely open, my tongue unleash itself. Curse and ruin to you who betrayed your God, you who are as unfaithful to the earthly Mary as to the heavenly one, to you who have sold yourselves to this Bastard Queen! ...Holy Mary, pray for me, and take me to you in your heavenly life. Mary, my Queen, pray for me. And embrace me when I meet you again in Heaven.

Exit MORTIMER, gun in hand. Voices, among them LEICESTER'S. Gunshot.

Scene Two

ELIZABETH'S office. Enter ELIZABETH and BURLEIGH.

ELIZABETH To lead me there! To manipulate me with such mockery! The traitor pig!

BURLEIGH I still cannot grasp by what power, what magic art he so well managed to surprise the wisdom of my Queen.

ELIZABETH I die for shame. I am severely punished for ignoring your wise advice. Who can I trust if he betrays me!

BURLEIGH   And he betrayed you to this false Queen from Scotland.

ELIZABETH   She will pay me for it with her blood. Has the sentence been drafted?

BURLEIGH   It is ready.

ELIZABETH   She will die. He will see her fall and fall after her. He shall be a monument to my severity, as once he was the proud example of my weakness. Take him to the Tower. He shall bear the full weight of its law.

BURLEIGH   He will push himself on you, to justify himself.

ELIZABETH   How will he justify himself? Does that letter not convict him?

BURLEIGH   You are mild and merciful. To see him, his strong presence, his persuasiveness–

ELIZABETH   I will not see him, never again. Have you given the order that he not be allowed if he comes?

BURLEIGH   It has been given, my Queen.

Enter LEICESTER.

ELIZABETH   I will / not see him!

BURLEIGH attempts to push LEICESTER out and fails.

BURLEIGH   Out! / Out! You are not allowed here! Stay out!

LEICESTER   Burleigh! Elizabeth! Burleigh! Ah! I want to see the insolent one who turns me away. If she is visible to a Burleigh, so is she to me!

BURLEIGH   Lord Traitor from Leicester, the Queen has forbidden you to see her. You are very bold to storm in here without permission.

LEICESTER   You are very cheeky, Sir, to say so. There is no one from whose mouth Lord Leicester is given permission or denial.

ELIZABETH   Out of my sight you unworthy traitor!

LEICESTER   Queen. My Elizabeth.

ELIZABETH   Speak! Heighten your crime! Deny it!

LEICESTER   Dismiss this irritant first.

ELIZABETH   Stay!

LEICESTER   He goes, and I will need only two moments to make you understand.

ELIZABETH   You hope in vain to manipulate me with your cunning.

LEICESTER   I only want to speak to your heart, and what I would entrust to your daring graciousness I also want to justify only to your heart.

ELIZABETH   Shameless! Give him the letter!

BURLEIGH hands LEICESTER the letter, which LEICESTER snatches and tosses aside.

LEICESTER It would appear to stand against me, I know, but I hope that I will not be judged by appearances.

ELIZABETH Can you deny that you were secretly corresponding with the Stuart!

LEICESTER My conscience is free. I confess that what she writes is true.

BURLEIGH His own mouth condemns him!

LEICESTER It was wrong, I admit, to keep this step a secret from you. I played a dangerous game. The world knows I hate the Stuart. I, who have been distinguished above all others by your favor, am right to take a daring course in pursuit of my duty!

BURLEIGH Duty? Why, if the course was good, did you conceal it?

LEICESTER You are used to prattling before you act, and are the town bell of your own deeds. That is your way, sir. Mine is to act first, and then to speak.

BURLEIGH You speak now because you must, Lord Leicester.

LEICESTER *(measuring him proudly)* And you boast of a wondrous, mighty deed, that you have saved the Queen, have exposed the treachery. Nothing can escape your sharp eye, you think. Yet despite all your insightful powers of detection, Mary Stuart would have been freed today had I not stopped it.

BURLEIGH Had you?

LEICESTER Yes, I! The Queen confided in Mortimer. She went even further. She gave him a bloody order to assassinate Mary. Is that not so?

BURLEIGH and ELIZABETH look at one another.

LEICESTER Is that not so?! Where were your thousand eyes that they did not see how this Mortimer deceived you? That he was a raging papist and a fanatic who came to free the Stuart and murder the Queen of England! Ha? It was through him, who smuggled the correspondence between Mary and I, that I learned about this plot. Today she was to have been ripped out of her prison. Just this moment I found out from his own mouth. I had him taken prisoner and in despair, his work having been overturned and his mask ripped off, he killed himself.

BURLEIGH Just now this happened?

LEICESTER / Yes now.

BURLEIGH Now, in this moment, / after I left you?

LEICESTER In this moment. / Yes.

BURLEIGH You say he killed himself! Not you him? Not you him?

LEICESTER Who was it then that saved you? Who was it? Burleigh?! Did he know the danger that surrounded you? No! It was me! Your faithful Leicester was your good angel!

BURLEIGH This Mortimer died quite conveniently for you!

ELIZABETH I don't know what I should say. I believe you, and I don't believe you. Oh that hateful woman who caused me all this agony!

LEICESTER ...She must die. Mary Stuart must die. And I insist that the sentence be immediately enforced.

BURLEIGH You insist? You advise this?

LEICESTER Yes, I advise it, Burleigh! As much as it disgusts me to grasp for an extreme, I see now, and I believe, that the welfare of the Queen calls for this bloody victim.

BURLEIGH Well. Since my Lord so faithfully and earnestly says it, I suggest that the execution of the sentence be transferred to him.

LEICESTER ...To me?

BURLEIGH To you. Surely a better means could not be found to shake off the suspicion that still rests on you than to administer that she whom it is said you love be beheaded.

ELIZABETH My Lord advises well. So be it, and so it stays. Bring me the Order to sign.

Exit BURLEIGH. Exit LEICESTER.

Scene Three

ELIZABETH'S office, shortly later. ELIZABETH and BURLEIGH.

ELIZABETH ...What is it?

BURLEIGH The people.

ELIZABETH What do they want, the people?

BURLEIGH A panic has already spread to London that an attempt on your life has been made, that murderers commissioned by the pope attacked you, that the Catholics have sworn to rescue Mary Stuart from prison and proclaim her queen. Your loyal people believe it, and are angry. Only her head will quiet them. Today must be her last. We must take care of it.

Enter DAVISON with an official document folder.

ELIZABETH What do you have there, Davison?

DAVISON What you have ordered, your Majesty.

ELIZABETH takes the folder. Enter SHREWSBURY.

BURLEIGH ...Obey the voice of the people, it is the voice of God.

ELIZABETH And who will tell me then whether it is the voice of all the people, of the entire world, that I hear. I am afraid that if I obey now the wish of the crowd, that a completely different voice will then make itself heard. Yes, and that the very men who now drive me by force to this action may, once it is taken, fiercely condemn me!

SHREWSBURY They wish to rush you, your Majesty. Be strong, stand firmly. I see that unfortunate paper in your hand. Do not read it.

ELIZABETH I am forced to.

SHREWSBURY Who can force you? You are the Queen of England. Command those raw voices that have the audacity to force your royal will, that would govern your judgment, to be silent. Only fear moves the people. You are not yourself at this moment, you are ill prepared. You are a human being. And right now you cannot make a judgement.

BURLEIGH This is not a judgement to be made, but to be executed. The people will no longer be controlled. I beg you, do not hesitate any further.

ELIZABETH You see, how they push me.

SHREWSBURY Collect your mind. Wait for a quieter moment.

BURLEIGH Wait! Hesitate! Delay! Until the empire stands in flames! Until the enemy finally succeeds at its murder game! Three times they have come close! To hope for one more miracle would be to tempt God!

SHREWSBURY That God, who has protected you four times, deserves trust. I will not raise the voice of justice now. Now is not the time. You cannot hear it in this storm. But please hear just this. You tremble now before the living Mary Stuart. It is the dead Mary Stuart that you have to fear. Tremble before the dead, the beheaded. She will rise from the grave a goddess of discord. When you have done this bloody thing, then go through London, show yourself to your people, which until now have swarmed jubilantly around you, and you will see another England, another people, because you will no longer be wrapped in the glorious righteousness with which you once conquered their hearts. Fear is the terrible ally of tyranny; it will shudder before you and desolate every street where you go.

ELIZABETH I am weary of this life, and of this crown! One Queen must fall, and thereby the other live! And there is nothing else that I know of now! And can I not be the one who yields? Then every dispute would end! God is my witness, that I have never lived for myself! Only for my people have I lived! I have ruled this island happily for many years, because I only needed to make people happy! Now comes my first serious kingly duty, and I feel my powerlessness!

BURLEIGH ...Now by God! You say you love your country more than yourself! Prove it now! Do not choose peace for yourself and cast a storm over the empire! Think of the church! Should the old superstitions return with this Stuart? The monk rule anew? Should the Catholic from Rome march in, close our churches, dethrone our monarchy? I demand of you the souls of all your subjects! How you act now, they are saved or they are lost! Here, as Shrewsbury has saved your life, so I will save England! That is more!

ELIZABETH Leave me to myself.

ALL begin to depart.

ELIZABETH Davison, you can stay nearby.

ALL exit. SHREWSBURY lingers longest, regarding ELIZABETH significantly before he goes.

Scene Four

ELIZABETH alone.

ELIZABETH ...Oh. The slavery of the public service. How tired I am of this idol of flattery that my inmost soul despises. I must respect opinion. Maneuver around praise. Appease a mob that only likes entertainment. One who must please the world is not yet a king. It is only one who in acting does not need to ask for the applause of humankind. Were I tyrannical, like my predecessor on this throne, I could now shed royal blood without rebuke. But is it now by my own choice that I am to be just? Omnipotent Necessity, which forces even the free will of Kings, made this virtue necessary to me. I want... I want to have peace. Her head must fall. She is the fury of my life! Mary Stuart! A plague to me, a ghost that destiny has chained to me! You must go, go, go, go, go! ...If she is blown out of the living, I am free, like the air on the mountain.

ELIZABETH signs the order.

ELIZABETH Davison!

Enter DAVISON.

ELIZABETH This paper. Take it back. I put it in your hands.

DAVISON takes the order.

DAVISON You have decided.

ELIZABETH I was supposed to sign it, and I have done so. A sheet of paper can decide nothing. A name does not kill.

DAVISON ...Your name, my Queen, on this paper decides everything. This paper orders that the death of the Queen of Scotland be announced, and that the execution take place at dawn. There is no clause for postponement. She is dead, if I deliver this paper.

ELIZABETH God has put a matter of great importance in your little hands.

Pray to him that he enlighten you with his wisdom. I go, and leave you to your duty.

DAVISON W– No, wait, don't leave. Not until you have told me what you want. Have you put this in my hands for me to deliver it so that the order is carried out?

ELIZABETH That you will do according to your wisdom.

DAVISON N–, no! Commands are my wisdom. Nothing here may be left to your servant. A small mistake here would be regicide. Explain to me in clear words your meaning: what should be done with this order?

ELIZABETH Its name speaks for itself.

DAVISON So, do you want for it to be executed?

ELIZABETH I did not say that. And tremble to think of it.

DAVISON Then you want me to hold onto it longer?

ELIZABETH At your own risk. You are liable for the consequences.

DAVISON I–? No, no! My God, what do you want?

ELIZABETH I want! That this matter should not be thought of anymore! That I finally have peace and am free of it forever!

DAVISON ...It takes a single word. Say what should be done with this paper.

ELIZABETH I have said. And now pester me no further.

DAVISON You haven't said anything to me!

ELIZABETH You are unbearable!

DAVISON Have patience with me. I only started here recently. I don't know yet the language used here. Please have patience with me. Clarify for me my duty... ...Take this paper back! Take it back! This is fire in my hands! Do not choose me to serve you in this terrible business!

ELIZABETH Do, what it is your duty, to do.

Exit ELIZABETH. DAVISON alone, not knowing what to do. Enter BURLEIGH.

DAVISON Here is the order. It is signed.

BURLEIGH Is it? Good. Give it to me.

DAVISON I can't. She did not make her wishes clear to me.

BURLEIGH Not clear? It is signed. Not clear. Give it here.

DAVISON carefully gives BURLEIGH the order. BURLEIGH checks it.

BURLEIGH So. Finally. Peace.

Exit BURLEIGH.

DAVISON Yes, free me from it.

Exit DAVISON.

Act Five
Scene One

MARY alone in the interrogation room, bound to the chair this time. It is clear the MARY has not slept.

MARY The end of my suffering nears. My prison opens up. My glad soul ascends to eternal freedom on angel wings. Benevolent, and healing, Death comes to me, like an earnest friend. With his black wings he covers my indignities.

I shall die in the hands of foreigners.

I have confessed all my earthly affairs, and hope to leave the world with no human debtors.

Stars, on the edge of eternity, it is the church, holy, high, that builds for us the ladder to the heavens. It is called the Catholic, universal, because it is only the universal faith that can strengthen faith. Where thousands worship and revere, there the embers become the flames, and the spirit is inspired to sweep up to the Heaven of all! The happy gather for the strengthening communal prayer in the House of the Lord. The altar is adorned, the candles shine, the bell sounds, the bishop stands, he takes up the cup, he blesses it, and declares the heavenly miracle of the metamorphosis, and the believing people fall down in the presence of God! In the name of the Father, and the Son, and the Holy Spirit!

Mary. Queen. Have you searched your heart? Do you swear, and do you vow, to confess the truth before the God of Truth?

My heart lies open here before you.

Speak, what sin pulls at your conscience since the last time you reconciled with God?

My heart was filled with envious hate, and vengeance raged inside of me. I hope for God's forgiveness that I could not forgive my enemy.

Do you regret this sin, and is it your earnest decision to leave this world reconciled?

Yes, yes. As truly as I hope God will forgive me.

What other sin does your heart charge against thee?

Not through hate alone, but through sinful love have I also insulted the highest good. My vain heart was drawn to the unfaithful man who abandoned and betrayed me.

Do you regret this sin, and has your heart turned from this vain idol to God?

It was the hardest struggle that I withstood. The last earthly bond is torn.

What other guilt petitions your conscience?

An early, bloody sin, long since confessed, that returns with terrible force in the moment of my last accounting, and unfurls blackness before the gates of Heaven. The king, my husband, I allowed to be murdered, and I gave my heart and hand to the seducer who murdered him! By strict penance I have made all atonements, but in my soul the worm will not sleep!

Does your heart charge you with no other sins that you have still not confessed and paid for?

No, no. You now know everything that burdened my heart.

Think on the presence of Omniscience. Think on the punishments with which the high church threatens mangled confessions, which are a sin to the eternal death, for they are a sin against the Holy Spirit!

So give me the grace of eternal victory in my last fight, as I have knowingly hidden nothing from you.

How? Will you conceal from your God the crime for which humanity punishes you? You tell me nothing of your bloody part in Babington's high treason, for which you die an earthly death. Do you also wish to die for it the everlasting death?

I have called upon everything I possess to free myself from undignified chains. But never have I through intent or deed attempted the life of my enemy.

...Blood can reconcile what blood has done. The blessed spirit does not follow the weaknesses of mortality in the Transfiguration. So receive the body that for thee was sacrificed.

MARY does.

MARY Receive the blood that was shed for your sins.

MARY does.

MARY And as you now in this earthly body have held mysterious communion with your God, so will you there in his joyful realm, where no more sins will exist, and no tears, as a beautiful, transfigured angel, unite yourself forever with God.

Scene Two

Enter BURLEIGH, PAULET, and LEICESTER, who remains to the side, unable to raise his eyes.

BURLEIGH   I come, Lady Stuart, to receive your last commands.

MARY   My Testament names my last wishes. And since my body shall not rest in consecrated ground, I ask that this loyal servant carry my heart to my relations in France.

BURLEIGH looks to PAULET, who nods.

BURLEIGH   It shall be done. Is there anything else?

MARY   Paulet. Let me hope that you will not think on me with hate.

PAULET   *(kindly)* Go in peace.

MARY   Her Majesty of England. Bring her my sisterly greeting. Say to her, that I forgive her for my death from my heart, and ask her with remorse to pardon the severity I showed her yesterday. God preserve her, and grant her a happy reign.

BURLEIGH unbinds MARY.

MARY   Now I have nothing more in this world. My savior, my redeemer, as you once spread your arms on the cross, so now open them to receive me.

BURLEIGH and PAULET start to lead MARY out. MARY sees LEICESTER now and looks at him for a moment before exiting with BURLEIGH and PAULET. LEICESTER remains behind.

LEICESTER   I live still. I still live. Does Heaven not crash down on me? Does the abyss not yawn to devour this wretched creature? What have I lost? What have I lost? I still live. Away from this house of horror and death. This head was a rock.

Exit LEICESTER.

Scene Three

ELIZABETH'S office. ELIZABETH alone. Enter PAULET.

ELIZABETH   You come alone? Where are the others?

PAULET   Lord Burleigh, and Lord Leicester–

ELIZABETH   –Where are they?

PAULET   They are–

ELIZABETH   –Where are they then?

PAULET I do not know where they are. I am told that Lord Leicester has left.

ELIZABETH She is dead. She is dead. She is dead. She is dead, she... Finally. Finally I have space on this earth! Ah! And who dares say I have done it?!

It is not clear whether ELIZABETH laughs or cries. Enter SHREWSBURY, hurriedly.

SHREWSBURY Your Majesty. Your Majesty, with concern in my heart for your name, I went to where Mary's house servant now sits in prison to test the truth of his testimony one more time. He lay in his cell like someone tormented by the Furies. No sooner did the miserable man see me than he implored me, begged me to tell him his Queen's fate, because rumors had reached the prison that she had been condemned to death. When I confirmed that the rumors were true, and then told him it was on his testimony that she would die, he leapt up wildly, then damned himself to hell. His testimony had been false.

ELIZABETH Hm.

SHREWSBURY The unlucky Mary's letter to Babington, which he had sworn was true, was false. He had written down words other than what the Queen had dictated. He ran to the window and clutched at the bars, and screamed out that he was the traitor who had falsely accused his mistress, he was damned, he was, yes, a false witness!

ELIZABETH You said yourself that he had lost his senses. The words of a frenzied madman prove nothing.

SHREWSBURY But yes, this madness itself proves there has been more. Let me beg you, not to be over hasty. Order a new investigation.

ELIZABETH ...I will do it. Because you wish it. Not because I can believe that my counselors judged this matter over hastily. To reassure you, the inquiry will be renewed. Luckily there's still time. Not a shadow of a doubt should rest on our honor. Davison! Davison! Davison! Davison!

Enter DAVISON.

ELIZABETH The sentence, sir, that I put in your hands, where is it?

DAVISON The sentence?

ELIZABETH That I put in your custody.

DAVISON In my custody?

ELIZABETH The people assailed me to sign it. I had to do their will. I did it. Forced, I did it. And in your hands I left the paper where is it?

SHREWSBURY The inquiry must be renewed.

ELIZABETH ...Don't ruminate on it. Where is the paper? ...I do not hope, Sir–

DAVISON –I– I'm– I don't have it anymore!

ELIZABETH How? ...What!

DAVISON It is in Burleigh's hands, since yesterday.

ELIZABETH Did I not strictly command you to keep it safe?

DAVISON You did not command that!

ELIZABETH Will you punish me with lies? When did I call upon you to give the paper to Burleigh?

DAVISON Not in precise, clear words, but–

ELIZABETH –You dare to interpret my words? To lay your own bloody meaning in them? Woe to you if some misfortune comes from this high-handed deed! You shall answer me for it with your life!

DAVISON Yes. Yes, your majesty.

Exit DAVISON. PAULET follows after him. Enter BURLEIGH.

BURLEIGH May all enemies of this country end like the Stuart.

SHREWSBURY covers his face with a hand. After a moment, ELIZABETH addresses BURLEIGH.

ELIZABETH Burleigh. Did you receive the death order from me?

BURLEIGH ...No, I received it from Davison.

ELIZABETH And did Davison give it to you in my name?

BURLEIGH No. He did not.

ELIZABETH And you carried it out, without my will? The sentence was just. The world can not blame us. But you do not have the right to presume the leniency of my heart. For that you are banished from my face.

Exit BURLEIGH.

SHREWSBURY Do not banish your loyal friends. Do not throw into prison those who acted for you, and now keep silent for you. Allow me, however, to give back to you the seal that for twelve years you entrusted to me.

ELIZABETH No, Shrewsbury. You cannot leave me now.

SHREWSBURY I could not save your nobler part. Live. Rule happily. The enemy is dead. From now on you have nothing more to fear. Or to respect.

Exit SHREWSBURY.

ELIZABETH remains alone.

The end.

Salomania

Salomania

Salomania was originally commissioned and produced by Aurora Theatre Company, Berkeley, CA. Tom Ross, Artistic Director. Julie Saltzman, Managing Director. The world premiere was given there on June 21, 2012. The production was directed by the author, with the following cast and staff:

MAUD ALLAN	Madeline H.D. Brown
SOLDIER #1 / JUSTICE WILLS / BILLING / THEO	Mark Anderson Phillips
SOLDIER #2 / MARGOT / EILEEN / ISABELLA / SARA	Marilee Talkington
SOLDIER #3 / OSCAR WILDE / HERBERT / DARLING / JUDGE MURPHY	Kevin Clarke
SOLDIER #4 / SPENCER / BUSINESS MAN	Anthony Nemirovsky
SOLDIER #5 / LORD ALFRED DOUGLAS / 2ND & 3RD GUARDS / BARTENDER	Liam Vincent
SOLDIER #6 / 1ST GUARD / HUME-WILLIAMS	Alex Moggridge
Choreography	Chris Black
Scenery	Nina Ball
Costumes	Callie Floor
Lights	Heather Basarab
Sound	Matthew Stines
Properties	Mia Baxter
Stage Manager	Amanda Krieger

Dramatis Personae

> *Maud Allan* – the Salome dancer.
> *Soldier #1* – knows what he thinks. The Honorable Justice Wills. Noel Pemberton-Billing. Theo Durrant.
> *Soldier #2* – a sensitive lad. Margot Asquith. Eileen Villiers-Stuart. Isabella Durrant. Sara.
> *Soldier #3* – has an "eye for Tommy." Oscar Wilde. Herbert Asquith. Judge Darling. Judge Daniel J. Murphy.
> *Soldier #4* – trigger happy. Spencer. Business Man.
> *Soldier #5* – eccentric and conservative. Lord Alfred Douglas. Second Guard. Third Guard. Bartender.
> *Soldier #6* – skeptical, but a good man. First Guard. Hume-Williams.

Set

A No Man's Land. The stage of London's Palace Theater. A trench made of mud and sandbags, with scraps of the Great War lodged into it here and there. A private office, various parties, and a breakfast room. A courtroom. A scaffold with a noose. A pub. A cafe table with two chairs. All this at once.

Notes

A slash in the dialogue (/) indicates that the next actor should start their line, creating overlapping speech.

A general note regarding music. In some instances a particular piece of music has been specified, while in others it is simply indicated, "Music." Sometimes music has not been indicated, though perhaps it should be used.

For the Aurora Theatre Company production, music choices for dances and underscoring were drawn largely from the various composers that Maud Allan is known to have danced or listened to. Sometimes the actual pieces she danced to were used, but also other pieces by those composers and their contemporaries. Sound was also used to sharply punctuate the various scene shifts, and the projection of titles. In any case, directors and sound designers should determine for themselves when and what music best suits their production.

Prologue

MAUD ALLAN enters and stands center, dressed for travel and holding two suitcases.

TITLE: "14 February, 1895. Maud Durrant moves from San Francisco to Berlin, Germany, to study music."

MAUD ALLAN drops her suitcases, surprised by shocking news.

TITLE: "Soon after, she changes her name to Maud Allan and abandons music to pursue a career in dance."

OSCAR WILDE enters and stands in court. LORD ALFRED DOUGLAS stands at a safe distance. MAUD ALLAN sees them both. As THE HONORABLE JUSTICE WILLS and FIRST GUARD now enter to take their places in the court, seeing them as well SHE picks up her suitcases and leaves hurriedly.

THE HONORABLE JUSTICE WILLS Oscar Wilde.

> TITLE: "25 May, 1895. In London, England, Oscar Wilde is convicted of practicing a love the name of which one dares not speak."

THE HONORABLE JUSTICE WILLS Oscar Wilde, the crime of which you are convicted is so bad that one must put stern restraint upon one's self to prevent from describing, in language I would rather not use, the sentiments which must rise in the breast of every man of honor who has heard the details of these terrible trials. You have been at the center of the most perverse, hideous, sickening circle of corruption of young men. I shall, under the circumstances, be expected to pass the severest sentence the law allows. In my judgement even that is totally inadequate for such a case as this. It is the worst case I have ever tried. The sentence of the court is that you be imprisoned and kept to hard labor for two years.

> *THE HONORABLE JUSTICE WILLS starts to leave.*

OSCAR WILDE And may I say nothing, my lord?

THE HONORABLE JUSTICE WILLS The court is adjourned.

> *THE HONORABLE JUSTICE WILLS exits.*

> *OSCAR WILDE turns and meets eyes with LORD ALFRED DOUGLAS, who tries not to attract attention to himself. The look between them is significant. FIRST GUARD starts to lead OSCAR WILDE away.*

> TITLE: "30 November, 1900. Having served his sentence, Oscar Wilde, now exiled and destitute, dies of cerebral meningitis in Paris, France."

> *MAUD ALLAN enters and takes her place center stage, now dressed to dance.*

> TITLE: "6 March, 1908. Maud Allan makes her London debut at The Palace Theater."

> *Music. MAUD commences her performance. It is bold, confident and proud. As the dance progresses, LORD ALFRED DOUGLAS exits. When MAUD's dance reaches its climax, all of London bursts into applause. A bouquet of red poppies drops from the sky and lands near her feet. MAUD picks it up.*

Scene One

At that very moment, bombs rain down from the sky and machine gun bullets cut through the air. MAUD runs for cover as SIX BRITISH SOLDIERS fly over the top of a trench and slide down into the mud below. The explosions cease. THE SOLDIERS catch their breath solemnly in the wake of it.

TITLE: "Spring 1918. A British trench in France."

Finally someone speaks.

SOLDIER FIVE ...Number twenty-three.

EVERYONE but SOLDIER TWO laughs ironically. Once the conversation gets rolling, every subject is handled lightly, briskly, passing the time as in the pub.

SOLDIER SIX ...What were we saying before?

SOLDIER FOUR Chocolate.

SOLDIER ONE This one was going on about the Dutch.

SOLDIER THREE Was I?

SOLDIER FIVE Something with an A?

SOLDIER THREE *(remembers:)* Alkalinization! Yeh, a Dutch bloke – van Houten, or something like that – discovered that the naturally acidic taste of cacao was neutralized if he added an alkaline substance to the nibs before they were roasted.

SOLDIER TWO What's a nib?

SOLDIER FOUR Sounds like a Chinaman.

SOLDIER THREE A nib is the kernel of a cacao bean, the basic ingredient of which all chocolate is made. All reputable chocolate makers now practice this alkalinization process to modify the flavor and color of their chocolate, in order to render it smoother in both respects. In that regard, I myself am particularly fond of Rowntree's of York. An exceptionally smooth chocolate. Leaves a lovely aftertaste, which is quite essential. A good aftertaste should leave positive flavors in the mouth for two minutes at least. I don't believe I would be going too far if I were to estimate that a decent square of Rowntree's might well linger in the mouth for up to three minutes. Perhaps longer.

SOLDIER FOUR I prefer the Cadbury chocolate bar, meself.

SOLDIER THREE I know that about you. And you're wrong.

SOLDIER FOUR I can't be wrong, it's a matter of taste, which as anyone knows is indisputable.

SOLDIER THREE You prefer the Cadbury chocolate bar due to its wrapper. And a wrapper, in fact, is not a matter of taste. A wrapper has no taste. What does have a taste is the chocolate to be found inside that wrapper. And in that regard I maintain that Cadbury is entirely inferior in all respects to Rowntree's of York.

SOLDIER SIX He's right. Anyway, your Cadbury with its British Flag wrapper is pure sensationalism.

SOLDIER FOUR Sensationalism?

SOLDIER SIX One can just as well buy a Cadbury in its basic wrapper. Neutral. With no concern beyond the sanitary transport of the chocolate itself.

SOLDIER FIVE I remember a Cadbury wrapper from before our summer of fourteen, on which a rather sporty chap was playing Cricket, sent to the boys fighting in Africa.

SOLDIER SIX A gentle reminder of the civilized way of life they were fighting for. What does old Cadbury send us? The bloody British flag? Cadbury would do well to wrap his bars in the Belgian flag; they say we're here for little Belgium, after all. Just wait till I get a hold of little Belgium.

SOLDIER THREE Good chocolatiers those little Belgians.

SOLDIER FIVE Really. I'm a Bovril man. Not too sweet. A touch bitter.

SOLDIER TWO I rather like A.J. Caley & Son meself.

SOLDIER SIX Brilliant. Another one.

SOLDIER THREE And so young.

SOLDIER SIX And why. Because the wrapper says – no: announces, "Active Service Chocolate?" Less romantic I suppose than Cadbury's flag, but hardly less subtle. A.J. Caley and his sticky fingered spawn are profiteering off your mum's patriotism.

SOLDIER ONE Nothing wrong with mum's patriotism, now is there.

SOLDIER FOUR Better not be, anyway.

SOLDIER THREE Gentlemen. It is the quality of the experience that is at issue. Rowntree's of York is in fact as close to a ganache as one can get in bar form: a rich, silky chocolate made from semisweet and boiled cream, stirred into velvet; sometimes flavored with fruits, spices, liqueurs. The result being a harmonious balance between the smoothness of the flavor, and the intensity of the chocolate. And it is just this ganache-like balance that Rowntree's of York achieves in even its most utilitarian bar.

SOLDIER ONE Do I recall correctly that before the war Rowntree's of York printed their wrappers in English, French, and also German?

SOLDIER THREE They did.

SOLDIER ONE Well then.

Some satisfied chuckles from ONE, FOUR and FIVE. A brief pause.

SOLDIER FOUR ...Number eighty-five.

EVERYONE but SOLDIER TWO laughs.

SOLDIER SIX ...I've grown rather partial to Lowney's Canadian Sweet Milk Chocolate meself.

SOLDIER TWO Oi. Where was it the Germans crucified that Canadian?

SOLDIER FOUR Ypres.

SOLDIER SIX The Somme.

SOLDIER FOUR Ypres. And he wasn't Canadian. He was British.

SOLDIER TWO I always heard it he was Canadian.

SOLDIER SIX The Yanks of course made it two Canadians. They'll do anything to make a story more spectacular.

SOLDIER FOUR It's not a story.

SOLDIER TWO There were two Canadians?

SOLDIER FOUR No. There was one, red-blooded, British soldier, crucified by Jerry and Fritz on a tree. They stood round him till he died, vile animals.

A pause while this is considered.

SOLDIER THREE ...All is quiet in No Man's Land.

SOLDIER FIVE ...Funny name, that. "No Man's Land." It's actually quite well populated when you stop to think about it.

THEY do.

SOLDIER TWO ...And what o' that wild regiment one hears about?

General appreciation from ONE, FOUR and FIVE about this next topic.

SOLDIER THREE *(not again:)* Oh God.

SOLDIER SIX What about it?

SOLDIER TWO Don't know. I've only heard dribs and drabs.

SOLDIER SIX Legend has it, and many believe, there is a regiment of men who live in the holes and caves beneath No Man's Land. French, German, British, Austrian, Canadian, Italian, a real international delegation. So high in number they would need to be exterminated. They slip out between stalemate battles to rob the dead of any rations or ammunition. That's how they get on. So the story goes.

SOLDIER TWO Has anyone ever seen them?

SOLDIER FOUR Sometimes you hear them. They sound like dogs.

SOLDIER ONE *(howls low like a distant dog)*

SOLDIER TWO How'd they get out there?

SOLDIER SIX Left behind.

SOLDIER FOUR Or thrown out.

SOLDIER TWO Thrown?

SOLDIER FOUR Maybe they shot off a finger, gripped the barrel of a hot MG. Some men will do anything for a Blighty One to buy their ticket home. They lose their nerve, go a bit mad and start taking unnecessary risks.

SOLDIER SIX What's an "unnecessary risk?" The maddest thing I ever did was under orders.

SOLDIER FOUR They aimed to desert, got their just deserts and were deserted. Now their home is the mist and mud of No Man's Land.

SOLDIER TWO Sounds like a ghost story.

SOLDIER SIX It is a ghost story.

SOLDIER FOUR I've heard'm.

SOLDIER FIVE So have I.

SOLDIER SIX Those were dogs.

SOLIDIER FOUR Well if they weren't dogs before they are now.

SOLDIER FIVE Living like dogs, anyway.

SOLDIER THREE Quiet! ...I think that's Mathilde.

A lark is singing and EVERYONE listens. SOLDIER THREE checks his watch.

SOLDIER THREE A bit early today. Mathilde usually sings nearer sunset. ...Beautiful.

SOLDIER SIX Makes all the rest seem quite silly, doesn't she?

Mathilde continues to sing.

SOLDIER THREE ...I prefer a good sunset to a sunrise. I used to prefer a sunrise. Something naive and uncomplicated about it, the way the light spreads indiscriminately across the sky. But there's a smoldering to sunset, kindled by experience.

Mathilde continues to sing.

SOLDIER THREE ...Now, a sunset at the sea is twice as experienced, and twice as smoldering, the sky and sea being ancient quarrelling lovers.

SOLDIERS ONE and FOUR exchange a glance in regard to THREE'S purple comment.

SOLDIER ONE ...Number twelve.

EVERYONE but SOLDIER TWO laughs.

SOLDIER TWO Oi. Why is it when someone says a number, everyone laughs.

SOLDIER SIX We've told the same jokes so often we decided to give them numbers, save ourselves the time.

SOLDIER TWO Really.

SOLDIER TWO considers. Finally:

SOLDIER TWO ...Number forty-six.

EVERYONE looks, but nobody laughs.

SOLDIER TWO Nobody laughed.

SOLDIER SIX Some people just can't tell a good joke.

SOLDIER TWO It's just a number.

SOLDIER SIX Might help in the delivery if you knew what it meant.

SOLDIER TWO Will you teach me?

SOLDIER SIX There are a lot of numbers.

SOLDIER TWO Come on.

SOLDIER SIX When Mathilde's finished.

Mathilde still sings for a bit. Music – Sibelius' "Valse Triste."

MAUD has entered, as if on stage, and now dances to the music. THE SOLDIERS also dance their inner lives. As the dance unfolds, the sun moves across the sky a bit. It's all quite beautiful.

When the dance is finished, EVERYONE is again as they were. MAUD is greeted by applause from a large audience. A newspaper drops from the sky and lands near her feet. MAUD opens the paper and reads something she doesn't like, then casts the paper to the ground and the applause ends abruptly. MAUD exits.

Scene Two

SOLDIER SIX This just in, men!

General appreciation and all shift in place for story time. SOLDIER SIX takes up the paper.

SOLDIER ONE What will *The Daily Mirror* reflect today?

SOLDIER THREE What's on the boards in London?

SOLDIER SIX Yes, I've got leave tomorrow. Let's see what's on.

SOLDIER FIVE Does Maud Allan have anything on?

SOLDIER ONE Not a stitch, probably.

Naughty laughter.

SOLDIER SIX Don't have to look too far for Miss Allan. Front page again.

SOLDIER THREE And what is the latest on the Cult of the Clitoris?

Naughty laughter again, with SOLDIER TWO laughing most.

SOLDIER FOUR You still don't know what it means, do you?

SOLDIER TWO Clitoris? Puh! Course I know it.

TWO's awkward forced laughter confirms otherwise.

SOLDIER FOUR Alright. What is it, then?

SOLDIER SIX Careful what you say. Wouldn't want any of Billing's lot to take you for one of the Forty-Seven Thousand, now would you? Why aren't any of us on the front page, that's what I want to know.

SOLDIER ONE Who wants to read about you? Either give us the latest on Allan and Billing or hand it over to someone who will.

SOLDIER ONE has his hand out.

SOLDIER SIX I find it increasingly difficult to shake off the feeling that this entire war has been written by someone. And all this business at the Old Baily with Maud Allan and Noel Pemberton-Billing is a farce meant to distract the civvies from the depressing portents of their Greek chorus – that being us lot – sent away to act our guts out as spear carriers on this blasted bleeding French heath. I thought that bloody, buggering bastard Lloyd George was going to get us out of what Asquith muddled.

SOLDIER FIVE One Prime Minister is like the next, the next like the last.

SOLDIER FOUR Just read the bloody headlines!

SOLDIER THREE Gentlemen, you will come to order.

SOLDIER SIX I can read it, but you'll never really know what's happening, will you, if you aren't actually there.

SOLDIER TWO You've got leave tomorrow.

SOLDIER SIX If I don't go under first.

SOLDIER TWO You could stop by the Old Baily, see Maud Allan in person, let us know firsthand.

SOLDIER FOUR Cut the chat and hand him *(i.e. SOLDIER ONE)* the bloody newspaper you lousy git. It's the only thing left in this world that gives my life meaning.

SOLDIER SIX What meaning does it give you to read about some half arsed dancer getting dragged through the mud by a greasy pack of lawyers and politicians, none of whom know what it is to wear your boots. Anyway it's nobody's business what she does behind her curtains. She dances, and rich men cross their legs. So what? Then she acted in a dirty play by that Oscar Wilde bloke for a bunch of perverts minding their own business. She's just trying to make a living off other people like anyone else.

SOLDIER ONE Or she's a traitor to England.

SOLDIER FOUR You know what he sounds like? A bloody conchie. You haven't turned conscientious on us, have you?

SOLDIER SIX Go on! Rather than reading this rot to you lot I'd do better to fold it up and stick it in a dry place, if I could find one, just in case I need something to wipe your arse when Fritz comes to give your life some real meaning.

SOLDIER FOUR Oh for god's sake, man! All I want is a little entertainment! Is that so much to bloody ask? For god's sake! Read the bloody fucking *Daily Mirror*! Just read it! Read it you bloody sod!

SOLDIER SIX *(to himself more than anyone)* How did we end up stuck out here, anyway? Who started all this shit?

> *SOLDIER SIX snaps open the paper.*

Scene Three

> *Sudden shift. SOLDIER ONE is now BILLING, and SOLDIER FOUR is now SPENCER, an American. The latter has just arrived in the former's office.*

> *Throughout this scene, other SOLDIERS respond with laughter, murmurs or other such things as appropriate. Perhaps this sort of thing happens throughout the play.*

SPENCER Billing.

> TITLE: "London. The private office of Noel Pemberton-Billing, British Member of Parliament and chief editor of The Vigilante."

BILLING Captain Spencer. Let's get right to it, shall we. What is this "New Plan?"

SPENCER Well: if the Germans are bestial Huns, as our and other responsible newspapers say, and the British are noble patriots fighting a noble cause, why are the Germans clearly winning? Why are German banks still allowed to keep their doors open in England? Why is a single German alien still permitted to live openly on British streets?

BILLING Because Lloyd George is no better a Prime Minister than that Hun-suckling Herbert Asquith before him.

SPENCER And yet there's nobody but Herbert Asquith in a position to replace Lloyd George.

BILLING A rather incestuous little club, isn't it.

SPENCER We know the two of them are in cahoots planning secret peace talks with Germany, against the express wishes of the War Office that, like us, wants to see this war through to its rightful end. And: neither of them have dealt properly with these Germans living in England.

BILLING Obviously they can't be depended upon to betray their friends. Or themselves. We have been publishing slanderous suggestions for nearly two years now without one libel charge brought against us. It's rather discouraging.

SPENCER Yes/–

BILLING –I need a public platform, outside of Parliament, to make our case, to the people, before this war ends as badly as it has gone!

SPENCER That is precisely the aim of my plan.

BILLING gestures for SPENCER to go ahead.

SPENCER Now: the tendency in Germany is to abolish civilization as we know it by infecting clean nations with the erotomania of Sodom and Gomorrah. That is a fact.

BILLING Yes.

SPENCER And, the blond beast being a deviant, he commands the deviants in other lands. They become his moles. They burrow. They plot. They're hardest at work when they're most silent. And at the moment, they're not saying a word.

BILLING *(impatient of the fact)* No.

SPENCER Our article should have earned you any number of libel cases. Everything I told you, that you printed for all to see, about the German Prince, his secret Black Book listing forty-seven thousand names of corruptible British Cabinet Ministers, wives of Cabinet Ministers, newspaper editors, diplomats, bankers, members of His Majesty's own household – all of this should have caused a scream. We need to help these forty-seven thousand traitors speak up. And it occurred to me, that concentrating our attention on one voice might prove more effective in the end than trying to conduct the entire chorus.

BILLING Who do you have in mind?

SPENCER hands BILLING an advertisement from a newspaper.

SPENCER Apparently, two private performances are being given of the play *Salome* by that degenerate Oscar Wilde. Do you know the play?

BILLING I've heard of it, of course.

SPENCER Why "private" performances?

BILLING The play is banned.

SPENCER The book can still be freely sold and read. Playing *Salome* in this production is Maud Allan. The dancer. American. Made her name and number here on a jig she called "The Vision of Salome."

BILLING I remember.

SPENCER Never saw it myself, but I hear she wore nothing at all, which is no surprise if you know she learned her craft in Berlin.

BILLING *(i.e. I'm with yuh, go on:)* Ah ha/...

SPENCER Nor can it be merely incidental that Maud Allan is known to be more than a casual acquaintance of the former Prime Minister, Herbert Asquith, and his wife – particularly the wife, if you follow me.

BILLING Margot Asquith has her reputation.

SPENCER And no reputation is earned without reason.

> *Shift. MAUD and MARGOT ASQUITH at a swell party. MARGOT is dressed in a Salome-like costume and has brought MAUD a drink.*

MARGOT ASQUITH Maud, darling!

MAUD ALLAN Margot!

> TITLE: "A society party, for ladies only, at the home of Margot Asquith, wife of the former Prime Minister, Herbert Asquith."

MARGOT ASQUITH How do I look?

MAUD ALLAN All the rage.

> *Polite but quite familiar cheek kisses. Their physicality in general remains rather familiar throughout.*

MARGOT ASQUITH Thank you ever so much for entertaining at our little party.

MAUD ALLAN I am absolutely delighted to have been asked.

MARGOT ASQUITH You were quite the sensation. All the ladies went mad for you. How did it feel performing to a room packed with unadulterated Salomaniacs?

MAUD ALLAN How did you convince their husbands to let them out of their houses alone and dressed like me?

MARGOT ASQUITH I couldn't say what their husbands are aware of or not.

MAUD ALLAN They will be soon enough. That pug-nosed woman from the *New York Times* was here, her limbs conspicuously covered. Though I do think

I noticed her wagging her tail just a bit.

MARGOT ASQUITH By the time whatever she writes makes it to America and back, I have no doubt that something infinitely more interesting will have transpired than what some husbands' wives did or did not wear to a party!

    THEY *laugh.*

MARGOT ASQUITH Maud, will you be staying with us tonight or going home?

MAUD ALLAN *(not without suggestion:)* Ask me that again after I've had another of these.

    MAUD kisses MARGOT on the mouth before sipping her drink. THEY smile and glance about to make certain they weren't noticed by that pug-nosed woman from the NY Times, *then move off to join the other guests.*

    Shift. Billing's office.

SPENCER Maud Allan has a reputation herself. I understand she's rather outspoken and comes with quite a temper. Apparently she slapped Oscar Wilde's former boy, Lord Alfred Douglas, at Lady So-and-so's garden party once.

    Shift. Another party.

MAUD ALLAN Lord Alfred Douglas.

    TITLE: *"A garden party at the home of Lady So-and-so."*

LORD ALFRED DOUGLAS Maud Allan, is it?

MAUD ALLAN Don't be coy. I read what you wrote about me in that dreary magazine of yours.

LORD ALFRED DOUGLAS Did you?

MAUD ALLAN Perhaps my "American grit and bluff," as you call it, is the very daring that places my art beyond the narrow grip of your stiff upper lip.

LORD ALFRED DOUGLAS I hardly think.

MAUD ALLAN That is correct, you hardly do. I should think a writer so intimately schooled in the ways of Oscar Wilde would understand poetry in motion when he saw it.

LORD ALFRED DOUGLAS I have had nothing to do with Oscar Wilde, living or dead, for years.

MAUD ALLAN As I understand it you were once his "dearest of all boys."

    In response to that, LORD ALFRED DOUGLAS *whispers something in* MAUD's *ear that we, the audience, cannot hear:*

LORD ALFRED DOUGLAS *(whispers:)* And your brother, Madam, was a murderer.

MAUD slaps DOUGLAS hard across the face, or maybe throws her drink in it.

Shift. Billing's office again.

BILLING Can't blame her for doing that. I'd thump the buggering twit myself if ever I had the chance. Why did she?

SPENCER Don't know. Some gossip or another. I'm sure we could find out. In any case – and here we come to the hook and bait of my plan – she would no doubt take a good swing at us were we to print this in tomorrow's edition:

SPENCER hands BILLING a draft of something.

Shift. MAUD and MARGOT in morning dress at breakfast in the Asquith's parlor. MAUD is reading a newspaper. HERBERT ASQUITH soon joins them, also dressed for the morning.

MAUD ALLAN "The Cult of the Clitoris."

TITLE: "Morning in the Asquiths' parlor."

MARGOT ASQUITH No! Really!

MAUD ALLAN Yes, listen: "To be a member of Maud Allan's private performances in Oscar Wilde's *Salome* one has to apply at 9, Duke Street, Adelphi, W.C. If Scotland Yard were to seize the list of these members I have no doubt they would secure the names of several thousand of the first forty-seven thousand."

HERBERT ASQUITH Who wrote that?

MAUD ALLAN *(looking)* A Mr. Noel Pemberton-Billing of *The Vigilante*.

MARGOT ASQUITH Oh Herbert.

HERBERT ASQUITH Billing. Of course.

MAUD ALLAN A friend of yours?

HERBERT ASQUITH Hardly.

MAUD ALLAN Forty-seven thousand who!

HERBERT ASQUITH Characters in a fairy tale about some German Prince with a little black book that Billing's been screaming all over Parliament about. Best to let it go, Maud.

MAUD ALLAN Let it go? It's outrageous. I am a respected and respectable artist! Do you think I'm going to sit quietly and allow My Good Name to be sullied by some "vigilante" of the press?

MARGOT ASQUITH Now, Maud, remember when Oscar Wilde brought libel charges, and what then happened to him. Do put it out of you mind.

MAUD ALLAN No! It's my name, Margot! My name! ...It's the only name I have.

MARGOT ASQUITH ...You must admit, Maud. It is rather funny.

MAUD ALLAN What is?

MARGOT ASQUITH "The Cult of the Clitoris!"

> *MARGOT and HERBERT both laugh, along with SOLDIERS FIVE and SIX. MAUD does not but rather slams down the paper.*
>
> *Shift. BILLING and SPENCER.*

BILLING Very concise, Spencer.

SPENCER Like a bullet.

BILLING And what's this Clitoris? Some tropical plant?

SPENCER Eh. No. It's a medical term, known only to doctors and perverts. As you're not a doctor I'm relieved you didn't recognize it.

BILLING Very funny, Spencer, you're no doctor yourself that I'm aware of.

SPENCER So I went to one and asked. "Clitoris" is the name of a certain organ of the female anatomy.

BILLING Ah. And you want me to print that. In bold type? That's obscenity.

SPENCER I needed something for the headline that might arouse curiosity and inflame the passions of any moral pervert who might object to being publicly associated with so tropical a term.

BILLING And who might thus expose herself in a libel case as one of our forty-seven thousand traitors to England.

SPENCER You print that tomorrow morning and I think you'll have your libel case before afternoon tea. And both Lloyd George and Herbert Asquith will be forced to clear out, cut short their beloved peace talks, and make way for those of us who actually want to win this war.

> *BILLING shakes SPENCER'S hand.*

BILLING Let's go to print, shall we?

> *Shift. MARGOT and HERBERT ASQUITH in their parlor reading the morning papers.*

HERBERT ASQUITH Well, Margot, it appears Maud has gone ahead and sued Billing for civil libel.

MARGOT ASQUITH Oh dear.

HERBERT ASQUITH Now he'll never shut up.

MARGOT ASQUITH Can anything be done?

HERBERT ASQUITH About Maud, no. She does what she likes.

MARGOT ASQUITH Proud thing. She'll give Billing a good row.

HERBERT ASQUITH He's very clever. And even more determined. Maud should sue him for criminal libel, if it can be justified. That would mean the trial goes to the Old Baily and he could be put away. Although with a venue like that he could also cause a lot of trouble for the peace talks before he goes.

MARGOT ASQUITH What will you do?

HERBERT ASQUITH I'm not Prime Minister anymore.

MARGOT ASQUITH Herbert, don't be bitter.

HERBERT ASQUITH Don't worry, Margot. A man like Billing won't be allowed to command center stage for long.

HERBERT has an idea and starts to go.

MARGOT ASQUITH Where are you going?

HERBERT ASQUITH Hopefully to save England from Noel Pemberton-Billing.

MARGOT ASQUITH How?

HERBERT ASQUITH I think Hume-Williams owes me a favor.

Shift. BILLING and SPENCER in Billing's office.

BILLING Well done, Spencer, old boy.

SPENCER Don't thank me just yet. The Crown has sent Hume-Williams to represent Maud Allan.

BILLING Have they. Asquith and Lloyd George mean business.

SPENCER Do you still intend to represent yourself?

BILLING I may be no lawyer but I remain my own best spokesman. Anyway, Hume-Williams is good. But we're right.

SPENCER That hasn't done much for us so far.

BILLING Yes, but that was in the halls of Parliament with a pack of dusty MPs. Now we're in the halls of the Old Baily with Maud Allan, celebrity. A famous dancer and actress, a high profile MP, and the moral state of Britain. There won't be an empty seat in the house.

Enter a Mrs. EILEEN VILLIERS-STUART.

EILEEN VILLIERS-STUART Mr. Billing?

BILLING ...I am. How may I help you?

EILEEN VILLIERS-STUART Have I called on you at a poor time?

BILLING That might depend on your reason for calling.

EILEEN VILLIERS-STUART It's a rather private matter with regard to your – current situation.

BILLING Captain Spencer is my right hand here at *The Vigilante*.

EILEEN VILLIERS-STUART He seems a right man for the job. Nevertheless, Mr. Billing.

BILLING ...Spencer.

SPENCER Not too late, Billing. Lots of work to do tomorrow. *(to EILEEN:)* Evening.

SPENCER exits.

EILEEN VILLIERS-STUART American, is he?

BILLING Originally.

EILEEN VILLIERS-STUART If I were Christopher Columbus and had discovered America I would have taken very good care not to tell anyone.

BILLING Discretion does have its rewards. Spencer was a Captain in the British Secret Service, until he was invalided out of duty. He's an ally, like his former countrymen are now to us all. What might I do for you, Misss...?

EILEEN VILLIERS-STUART Eileen Villiers-Stuart.

BILLING is at once even more intrigued.

BILLING Ah. Yes.

EILEEN VILLIERS-STUART You did receive my letter, then.

BILLING Please accept my apologies for the delay in responding. I've been kept quite busy by my "current situation." But, here we are, now in person and in private. What is it that you wished to tell me?

EILEEN VILLIERS-STUART That I have seen the German Black Book.

BILLING You have?

EILEEN VILLIERS-STUART It was shown to me once by Neil Primrose, Herbert Asquith's / Chief Whip.

BILLING Herbert Asquith's Chief Whip, yes. Why? How? Neil Primrose died in action in Palestine last year. When did you meet with him?

EILEEN VILLIERS-STUART I told you that you would be interested in what I had to say.

BILLING Oh indeed, indeed; though I must ask why I am the beneficiary of your favor, and not Asquith himself or someone else closer to the wheel.

EILEEN VILLIERS-STUART My father once tried to save England from becoming a second Berlin, and was derided for his pains. Now he's dead. And I am determined to carry on his work. I've read your and Mr. Spencer's various articles in *The Vigilante*. And I am so glad you printed what you did about that Maud Allan. Of course you were sued for libel. A libel action is always a cloak of counterfeit innocence worn by the guilty.

BILLING Indeed.

EILEEN VILLIERS-STUART Truth be told, Mr. Billing, I do not consider you were nearly severe enough when you said the first forty-seven thousand. I should have written the first four-hundred seventy thousand. There are places here, not a hundred yards from my hotel, where the disgusting devices adopted by that filthy Oscar Wilde are hourly carried on. And considering the principle habitués in these places are men high up in naval and military circles, one must wonder how many of our State secrets are exposed there. If these people were to be properly smoked out our armies would no doubt be in much better condition than now.

BILLING No doubt whatsoever.

EILEEN VILLIERS-STUART I can help you, Mr. Billing, and I am fully prepared to do so in every way.

> *EILEEN has removed her hat to underscore this last point. Music. Unseen by them, MAUD steps forward and begins to dance a seduction. BILLING's doubt, among other things, is aroused.*

BILLING ...It's not often one meets so willing an ally so unexpectedly.

EILEEN VILLIERS-STUART I suppose it isn't.

BILLING The unexpected can bring good fortune. Or bad.

EILEEN VILLIERS-STUART Christopher Columbus expected India, and got America instead. Too bad for him his countrymen didn't have the good sense to hold on to that unexpected discovery.

BILLING True.

EILEEN VILLIERS-STUART It is not without some personal risk that I have made myself available to you, Mr. Billing. I do hope you appreciate that fact.

BILLING Mrs. Villiers-Stuart/.

EILEEN VILLIERS-STUART If you doubt my motives enough to risk losing the help of one who out of love for her country has already risked her reputation on your behalf – writing to you and calling on you at your office late at night and uninvited – then perhaps you are not quite as vigilant a patriot as your newspaper suggests.

BILLING Mrs. Villiers-/Stuart.

EILEEN VILLIERS-STUART I want only to see England win this war as soon as possible and by whatever means necessary, not to sink deeper into the mud of France under German boots. I could take you this very moment to a certain cafe on Duke Street, just off Manchester Square, where in a back room you would no doubt find some pathetic military or naval gentlemen of high ranking indulging in disgusting perversions with one lesbian, sodomite, foreigner or other deviant. Limbs entwined in unnatural positions beneath gilded mirrors and paintings of exotic erotomania! Lips gushing far more than they should between bouts of stolen kisses! In the mad embrace of carnal lust and blinded by the dark veils of ecstasy our nation's most sacred secrets are betrayed!

BILLING Mrs. Villiers-Stuart!

EILEEN VILLIERS-STUART Mr. Billing!

> *BILLING and EILEEN lunge into a mad embrace and kiss just as madly. The music and MAUD'S dance rise around BILLING and EILEEN as they tumble about wildly. Then, after BILLING and EILEEN have only just consummated their sudden passion, just as suddenly:*

EILEEN VILLIERS-STUART Mr. Billing! There is something I must tell you!

BILLING Right now?

EILEEN VILLIERS-STUART I am not here of my own will! I was sent in my capacity as a private detective with instructions to entrap and to compromise you in order to damage your character.

BILLING You were sent! By whom?

EILEEN VILLIERS-STUART The offices of Herbert Asquith and Prime Minister Lloyd George.

BILLING Oh, of course!

EILEEN VILLIERS-STUART I'll admit that I agreed at least in part out of a personal fascination, a desire to meet you. Everything else I've said is true. I have seen the German Black Book. I do believe that our country is amuck with traitorous perverts in thrall to Berlin! With every fiber of my being I believe it! And you would find those men of high ranking in that back room of that cafe on Duke Street – were you to go there! Asquith and Lloyd George had hoped I'd lure you there so that their minions could photograph you and publish terrible insinuations.

BILLING My God!

EILEEN VILLIERS-STUART But I won't help them any further. I do believe in everything you stand for. My only weakness was to agree to meet you in service to their treachery, rather than come to you entirely on my own.

BILLING And why should I trust you now?

EILEEN VILLIERS-STUART You can't, I know. But you must. And I will prove myself to you.

> *BILLING moves away. But:*

EILEEN VILLIERS-STUART If you expose me we're both ruined.

BILLING I have done nothing!

EILEEN VILLIERS-STUART We have both just done quite something. And that was not my duty. That was entirely me. Wanting you.

EILEEN goes to BILLING.

EILEEN VILLIERS-STUART ...Do not doubt me, Mr. Billing. I am here to help you. Now more than ever. I could not have gone on without telling you the truth. Let me help you. Take me into your confidence.

But BILLING resists EILEEN's attempt at a kiss for a moment, before then giving in. Then:

BILLING We have a lot to discuss.
EILEEN VILLIERS-STUART Indeed.

Followed by another, bigger kiss.

Scene Four

Shift. The Old Baily Central Criminal court.

SECOND GUARD Eh–hem! Please return to order, the court is now back in session.

TITLE: "29 May, 1918. Day One in the trial of Maud Allan v. Noel Pemberton-Billing at the Old Baily Central Criminal Court."

SECOND GUARD The honorable Sir Justice Darling presiding.
JUDGE DARLING Thank you, ladies and gentlemen; and gentlemen of the jury. And welcome back to the case of Maud Allan versus Noel Pemberton-Billing. Before I ask Miss Allan to return to the witness box for her cross-examination, I ask her counsel, Mr. Hume-Williams, if he indeed has no further questions to put to her?
HUME-WILLIAMS I do not at this time, my Lord. Thank you.
JUDGE DARLING Very well. Then, Mr. Billing, I presume you will now wish to cross-examine Miss Allan.
BILLING Indeed, my Lord. But first I would like to make a formal protest that you have been selected to try this case.
JUDGE DARLING I beg your pardon?
BILLING My reason is that I have, in my position as a public man and Member of Parliament, on many occasions criticized the atmosphere of levity which your Lordship has frequently introduced into cases you have tried. Based on the manner in which you have conducted yourself toward me thus far, I fear these criticisms must have come to your attention.

JUDGE DARLING I can assure you at once they have not. In any case, the fact that you may take an unfavorable view of me can be no reason why I should not try your case. For by that logic you might excuse every Judge in London.

Laughter in court.

BILLING My Lord–

JUDGE DARLING –I will hear no more of this, if you please. Do you wish to cross-examine Miss Allan or don't you?

BILLING I do.

JUDGE DARLING Very well. Miss Allan, if you would be so good as to return to the witness box.

Anticipatory music while MAUD crosses to the witness box, very slowly. Time seems to suspend. All eyes follow her every move. Then:

JUDGE DARLING Thank you, my dear. Mr. Billing.

BILLING Miss Allan, we heard in Mr. Hume-Williams' brief examination of you an account of your dancing career, beginning with your success at London's Palace Theatre.

MAUD ALLAN Yes.

BILLING Where did you receive your initial dance training?

MAUD ALLAN I did not train formally as a dancer, but rather a musician.

BILLING Where did you train?

MAUD ALLAN In Germany.

BILLING So: the inspiration for your dancing was acquired during your musical training in Germany.

MAUD ALLAN No.

BILLING You did dance your signature creation, "The Vision of Salome," while you were in Germany, did you not?

MAUD ALLAN I have returned to do so, yes.

BILLING In any case, your dancing is a German art, is it not.

MAUD ALLAN Not at all.

BILLING But this art was quite foreign to the British public before you brought it with you over the border from Germany?

MAUD ALLAN I was the pioneer of an art form, which I introduced to this country, yes. But it does not belong to Germany. It is entirely my own.

BILLING And the result of this introduction has been a financially successful career, providing you with a great many social connections as well, true?

MAUD ALLAN I socialize, as anyone does.

BILLING I would say you move among the highest of society. You have been invited to many well-known houses, is that not correct?

MAUD ALLAN I have enjoyed a number of very gracious invitations by very gracious people.

BILLING Were you ever graciously invited to 10 Downing Street, the home of Herbert Asquith and his wife, Margot Asquith?

MAUD ALLAN I have had that honor, yes.

BILLING Did you meet Margot Asquith there?

MAUD ALLAN Naturally, I was her guest.

BILLING Never met her anywhere else?

MAUD ALLAN Yes.

BILLING Privately? In your dressing room at the Palace Theatre, perhaps.

MAUD ALLAN No.

BILLING Never?

MAUD ALLAN Never.

HUME-WILLIAMS My Lord, Mr. Billing has introduced the names of third parties who are not on the list of agreed witnesses.

JUDGE DARLING Yes, Mr. Billing, mentioning their names in this way comes to calling these people, you know.

BILLING Is that necessary, my Lord?

JUDGE DARLING Naturally. Otherwise how can it be relevant? If you are going to suggest that Margot Asquith met privately with Miss Allan, in her dressing room or anywhere, then Mrs. Asquith must have the opportunity to verify whether she did or not.

BILLING I never thought Miss Allan would deny it.

JUDGE DARLING When asking a question, a lawyer must always be prepared for the answer.

BILLING I am not a lawyer.

JUDGE DARLING That much is clear. Proceed with your witness, Mr. Billing.

BILLING ...Miss Allan, have you brought this Prosecution about entirely on your own initiative or were you advised to bring it?

MAUD ALLAN I was not advised to *bring* it.

BILLING Are you quite aware that you could have brought your action against me in the Civil Court, rather than the Criminal Court?

MAUD ALLAN What difference does it make to you which Court it is?

BILLING Are you aware, Miss Allan, that it is in fact not allowed to use the Criminal Courts to clear one's name?

MAUD ALLAN My Counsel must know better than you.

BILLING And yet here we are. I – who as we've just established am no lawyer

– even I know that libels of a private nature may be tried in a civil court. Whereas The Old Baily, a criminal court, is reserved for libels that may provoke the libelled person to a breach of the peace. Do you intend a breach of the peace, Miss Allan?

MAUD ALLAN I intend to clear my name, and I am going to have my name cleared. And I am going to trust a British jury to do that and not let a man like you run me down.

BILLING Did your political friends, Herbert and Margot Asquith, advise you as to which Court should try your case?

HUME-WILLIAMS My Lord, / please!

JUDGE DARLING Mr. Billing, I have just said, you may not mention such names unless you intend to call them as witnesses. Nor should you make implications you do not plan to substantiate with their testimony.

BILLING ...Let us turn now to the headline of the paragraph printed in *The Vigilante*, for which this alleged libel charge has been brought against me. Did you understand this headline, Miss Allan, when you read it?

MAUD ALLAN Yes.

BILLING Are you a doctor?

MAUD ALLAN No.

BILLING A medical student?

MAUD ALLAN No.

BILLING Have you read medical books?

MAUD ALLAN One is taught physiology in school.

BILLING Are you particularly acquainted with the term "clitoris?"

MAUD ALLAN Not particularly, Mr. Billing. But I know what one is.

BILLING Did you show this headline to your friends when you read it?

MAUD ALLAN There were some friends present, yes.

BILLING Did they understand the term?

MAUD ALLAN Yes.

BILLING Were they medical students?

MAUD ALLAN I am not a medical student, Mr. Billing, I have said; and I do not socialize with any that I am aware of.

BILLING Are you aware, Miss Allan, that out of twenty-four professional men to whom I have shown this term, only one of them, a doctor, understood what it meant?

MAUD ALLAN I cannot account for what any number of professional men understand about a woman's clitoris, Mr. Billing.

BILLING But you understand it.

MAUD ALLAN Yes, Mr. Billing, for although I am no medical student, I am a woman. How did you reach your understanding of a woman's clitoris, Mr. Billing?

BILLING Miss Allan, –

JUDGE DARLING Once again, Mr. Billing, you must not bring in the names of third parties unless you plan to call them as witnesses.

BILLING I have not brought in the name of any third party, my Lord.

JUDGE DARLING Who then is this Greek chap, Clitoris? Belonging to some woman or another?

BILLING ...I'll touch on that a bit later, my Lord.

JUDGE DARLING See to it that you do.

BILLING holds up a thin book.

BILLING Miss Allan, do you recognize this book?

MAUD ALLAN It is *Salome*.

BILLING By whom?

MAUD ALLAN Oscar Wilde.

BILLING *Salome*, by Oscar Wilde.

At BILLING'S signal, the SECOND GUARD distributes copies to MAUD and JUDGE DARLING.

BILLING Are you quite aware of what the late Mr. Wilde has written here?

MAUD ALLAN I am, having performed the title role, as you know.

BILLING Did it occur to you in studying the play that it depicts an incestuous sexual lust taking place between Herod and the child, Salome?

MAUD ALLAN Not at all.

BILLING Would you kindly read the lines that are marked.

MAUD ALLAN "Why does Herod look at me all the while with his mole's eyes under his shaking eyelids? It is strange that the husband of my mother looks at me like that. I do not know what it means. Of a truth I know it too well."

BILLING Is that not a reference to incestuous lust?

MAUD ALLAN Hardly. Salome is an innocent child who despises everything that is ugly and uncouth. Only the beautiful, pure and spiritual appeal to her.

BILLING Do they? She says that the moon is cold and chaste.

MAUD ALLAN Yes, and therefore good to see. "How good to see the moon. She is cold and chaste. She has the beauty of a virgin. She has never defiled herself. She has never abandoned herself to men."

BILLING A little later on page twenty-seven she says the moon is like a mad woman.

MAUD ALLAN She does not say that. Herod does.

BILLING checks page twenty-seven.

BILLING Herod does?

MAUD ALLAN Herod, a man, says that she is mad.

JUDGE DARLING That is correct. He says it right here.

BILLING Miss Allan, would you please read to the Court the next lines marked, spoken by Salome herself.

MAUD ALLAN "I am amorous of thy body, Iokanaan!"

BILLING That is a "spiritual" statement?

MAUD ALLAN To be amorous is a pleasing thing, is it not? Besides, her response to Iokanaan is not actually physical at all. His body is an embodiment of his spiritual passion. It is his spiritual passion that enters her soul; and she feels it, deeply.

JUDGE DARLING Go on.

MAUD ALLAN "Thy mouth is like a band of scarlet on a tower of ivory. It is like a pomegranate cut in twain. The pomegranate flowers that blossom in the gardens of Tyre, and are redder than roses, are not so red. The red blasts of trumpets that herald the approach of kings, and make afraid the enemy, are not so red. Thy mouth is redder than the feet of him who cometh from a forest where he hath slain a lion, and seen gilded tigers."

JUDGE DARLING Gilded tigers?

MAUD ALLAN Gilded tigers.

JUDGE DARLING Go on.

MAUD ALLAN "Thy mouth is like a branch of coral that fishers have found in the twilight of the sea, the coral that is kept for kings! There is nothing in the world so red as thy mouth. Suffer me to kiss thy mouth."

BILLING Eh–hem; do you not think that these lines suggest a graphic act of sexual lust?

MAUD ALLAN Well. You could say "Mary had a little lamb," and read into it a good many things if you like.

BILLING Can you tell me how an innocent child says such things and means them in a spiritual manner and not a carnal one? "Suffer me to kiss thy mouth." "I will kiss thy mouth." There are three pages of that.

MAUD ALLAN Have you never wanted to touch anything beautiful, Mister Billing? It is a natural desire.

BILLING You tell us there is no unnatural lust in her desire to kiss his mouth at all, when in the end she does kiss the decapitated head of John the Baptist and bites through his lips.

MAUD ALLAN She does not.

BILLING "Thou wouldst not suffer me to kiss thy mouth, Iokanaan. Well! I will kiss it now. I will bite it with my teeth as one bites a ripe fruit."

MAUD ALLAN She says "I will bite it." Not that she has bitten it.

BILLING Did you bite the lips in performance on stage!

MAUD ALLAN She does not bite the lips!

BILLING Then why does it say a few lines further on, "I have kissed"?

MAUD ALLAN Kissed! Not bitten!

BILLING "I have kissed thy mouth, Iokanaan, I have kissed thy mouth. There was a bitter taste on thy lips. Was it the taste of blood?"

MAUD ALLAN "Nay. But perchance it was the taste of love. ...They say that love hath a bitter taste. But what matter?" What matter.

BILLING Oh but it does matter, Miss Allan. It matters very much.

JUDGE DARLING How, Mr. Billing?

BILLING Are you aware, Miss Allan, of the life of Oscar Wilde? That he was a great moral pervert?

MAUD ALLAN I am acquainted with his lawsuit, if that is what you mean.

BILLING Would you say that anything in the tragedy of *Salome* makes an appeal to moral perverts?

MAUD ALLAN Nothing in the tragedy of *Salome* makes any appeal to moral perverts.

HUME-WILLIAMS My Lord, what is the point of all this?

BILLING It is my defense that this play ministers to moral perverts, and I think the onus is upon me, with regard to the libel brought against me, to prove that this woman is in fact ministering to moral perverts who live in this country and undermine its will. I am defending myself in the public interest.

HUME-WILLIAMS With great respect, I object entirely to the statement that Mr. Billing defends himself in the public interest.

JUDGE DARLING You must explain that, Mr. Billing.

BILLING I am endeavoring to do so. Are you aware, Miss Allan, that there are people in this country today who practice unnatural vices?

MAUD ALLAN There are such people everywhere, but I am not responsible for them.

BILLING You do know the biting of lips is an act of sadism.

MAUD ALLAN I do not know that.

BILLING Have you ever studied sadism, Miss Allan, and can you tell me what sadism means?

HUME-WILLIAMS My Lord–!

BILLING The paragraph which I published explicitly suggests that this play appeals to moral perverts of all kinds; and I respectfully submit that not only is the witness familiar with moral perversities, but, through the performance of this play, is catering to and promoting such perversities in this country, whether consciously or unconsciously.

JUDGE DARLING Oh no, it must be consciously. If it is unconsciously, then the indecency is only in the mind of the person who suggests it.

MAUD ALLAN Ha! ...I'm sorry, Mr. Billing, you were suggesting.

BILLING Miss Allan, do you consider it in the interests of our nation that Oscar Wilde's *Salome* be produced when we are in the midst of a great and terrible war?

MAUD ALLAN War and art have nothing to do with one another, Mr. Billing.

BILLING Does this play help us to concentrate our attention on the great national problem facing every British citizen today?

MAUD ALLAN It helps us to find solace in the beauty of art.

BILLING Do you mean to suggest that this play brings solace to the wives, daughters and sisters of three million men fighting in France?

MAUD ALLAN Were they allowed to see the play, it might.

BILLING And you would wish it that all these women who love their men should have their men's heads cut off?

MAUD ALLAN Oh dear God! I did not write the play!

BILLING But you acted in it!

MAUD ALLAN Does that make me the part, because I acted it? Of course not! Don't make a fool of yourself!

Good point. A few chuckles leveled at BILLING confirm this.

BILLING ...Miss Allan.

MAUD ALLAN ...Yes?

BILLING Miss Maud Allan. Is that your full name since birth?

MAUD ALLAN ...It is part of my name.

BILLING Will you tell the court your full name?

MAUD ALLAN ...Maud Allan Durrant.

BILLING hands MAUD another, thicker book.

BILLING Would you please turn to the page that has been marked.

MAUD does as asked, is visibly shaken by what she sees there and closes the book.

MAUD ALLAN I ask what this has to do with the case?

JUDGE DARLING May I see this book?

SECOND GUARD takes the book to JUDGE DARLING, or MAUD hands it to him.

BILLING I am reluctantly obliged to refer to this, my Lord.

HUME-WILLIAMS Reluctantly obliged!

JUDGE DARLING looks at the marked page in the book, then at MAUD, then to BILLING.

JUDGE DARLING ...Mr. Pemberton-Billing. Are you truly bound to ask this question?

BILLING I deeply regret it, but I am.

HUME-WILLIAMS May I see this book, my Lord?

SECOND GUARD brings the book to HUME-WILLIAMS.

HUME-WILLIAMS ...This is a most cruel proceeding on the part of the Defendant.

JUDGE DARLING It is not a question of whether it is cruel. Do you have any legal objection to it?

HUME-WILLIAMS It can have no bearing on this case.

JUDGE DARLING I am bound to say I cannot exclude it on any legal ground. You may put the question if you desire it, Mr. Billing.

Music. BILLING takes the book from HUME-WILLIAMS and holds it up to MAUD.

BILLING Could you please read the name of this book, Miss Allan Durrant?

MAUD ALLAN "Celebrated Criminal Cases of America."

BILLING Are you the sister of Theodore Durrant?

MAUD ALLAN I am.

BILLING Was your brother executed in San Francisco for murdering two young girls in the belfry of a church and outraging them after their deaths?

MAUD ALLAN ...My Lord–

JUDGE DARLING –You had better split it up. You see it involves several questions.

BILLING Yes, my Lord. Was your brother executed in San Francisco?

MAUD ALLAN Yes.

BILLING What was his crime?

MAUD ALLAN You have said what the crime was.

BILLING The murder of two young girls?

MAUD ALLAN Yes.

BILLING And outraging them after their deaths?

MAUD ALLAN Yes.

BILLING And their bodies were found in the belfry of a church?

MAUD ALLAN Yes.

BILLING I will now read from *The San Francisco Chronicle*, an American newspaper, dated November 9, 1895. "As Durrant turned to exit the court, his mother cried out, 'My boy! My darling boy!' and, throwing herself upon him, pressed her lips to his and clung to him passionately. When the guard managed to part them, it could be seen that, so forcefully had the mother kissed her son's lips, she had drawn blood."

> *MAUD rises from the witness box as if in a trance and begins to move through the space. When she speaks it is more for herself than for others.*

BILLING I do not need to point out the similarities between this incident and the events depicted in Mr. Wilde's play, in which you elected to perform and upon which you had already created the dance that made you famous.

MAUD ALLAN I'd never read that.

BILLING I am sorry to have had to read it to you. But you see it is known that sadism, incest and other such moral perversions are often hereditary.

HUME-WILLIAMS My Lord, this is ridiculous!

JUDGE DARLING You will need to prove that, Mr. Billing.

BILLING I intend to prove it, my Lord. I have witnesses listed who will do so. Miss Durrant.

MAUD ALLAN Allan. Maud Allan.

BILLING Miss Allan, do you still say that in depicting Salome's unnatural lust you did not risk inciting moral weakness in my countrymen?

MAUD ALLAN She loved him with the pure love that any girl would love another person. She loved the beauty and the passion of this man. And she felt the agony of *this* man's insults when he took her for a wanton and a harlot, which she was not.

BILLING Do you wish the Gentlemen of the Jury to understand–

MAUD ALLAN –I wish them to understand that Salome was not a perverse young woman: therefore Mr. Billing has no right to talk of sadism. I am not the first woman to play the role of Salome and I doubt I shall be the last!

BILLING Which do you think will do more harm to the moral fiber of this country, the witnessing of such a play or reading that little paragraph I wrote?

MAUD ALLAN That paragraph you wrote. Look what it has done already.

BILLING Miss Allan. ...Miss Allan.

JUDGE DARLING Miss Allan?

HUME-WILLIAMS Miss Allan.
SECOND GUARD Miss Allan?
SOLDIER FOUR Miss Allan.
BILLING Miss Allan!

Scene Five

> *Shift. THEO DURRANT stands before JUDGE DANIEL J. MURPHY. THIRD GUARD stands nearby, as does ISABELLA DURRANT.*

JUDGE DANIEL J. MURPHY Theodore Durrant.

> TITLE: "November 8, 1895. San Francisco. Theodore Durrant is convicted of murder in the first degree."

JUDGE DANIEL J. MURPHY Theodore Durrant, the crime of which you are convicted is so bad that I must put stern restraint upon myself to prevent from describing the sentiments that must rise in the breast of anyone who has heard the terrible details of this trial. These two women, young and inexperienced, put their trust in you as an upstanding member their church congregation, and for that you repaid them with the most perverse, hideous, and sickening betrayal. I shall, under the circumstances, be expected to pass the severest sentence the law allows. In my judgement even that is totally inadequate for such a case as this. It is the worst case I have ever tried. The sentence of the court is that you be hanged by the neck until dead.

ISABELLA DURRANT & MAUD ALLAN Ah!

THEO And may I speak, your honor?

JUDGE DANIEL J. MURPHY The court is adjourned.

> *JUDGE DANIEL J. MURPHY exits.*

ISABELLA DURRANT My boy! My darling boy!

> *ISABELLA throws herself around THEO and kisses him full on the mouth. She is pried away by the THIRD GUARD. The kiss was so forceful that it has cut THEO's lip and left blood both there and on ISABELLA's lips as well.*

MAUD ALLAN Theo!

> *MAUD moves as if she would fly across the Atlantic and into the arms of THEO, who ascends the scaffold with the assistance of the THIRD GUARD.*

ISABELLA DURRANT No! Maud! My dearest Maud. I hope this letter reaches you soon enough. Your brother is innocent. We all know it. Yet he had already been condemned by the press and this godforsaken city of rumor mongers long before that jury did the same! They call it the Crime of the Century. But Theo is not guilty and we shall prove it still!

MAUD ALLAN Mother–!

ISABELLA DURRANT –For your part, Maud, stay in Berlin.

MAUD ALLAN But Mama–!

ISABELLA DURRANT Do not come back under any circumstances. It would only make Theo feel he was the cause of blighting your prospects and you do not want him to feel any worse than he must.

THEO Maud?

MAUD ALLAN *(uncertain)* Theo?

ISABELLA DURRANT Write him.

THEO Maudie?

ISABELLA DURRANT Tell him you will study all the harder to do him proud.

MAUD ALLAN Theo!

ISABELLA DURRANT Do it, now! It is my wish, and his, that you remain in Berlin at all costs. So: sit up straight, no round shoulders. Take care of your health and your looks and your grammar. Stay out of harm. And do as Mama asks.

MAUD ALLAN But–!

ISABELLA DURRANT *(a warning:)* I know that you will. I am very proud of you, Maud. Love, your mother.

> *THEO is now atop the scaffold. The music has stopped and we hear a wind sweeping gently across a quiet No Man's Land. THIRD GUARD pulls out a pocket watch and we can hear its steady ticking.*

MAUD ALLAN ...Dear, dear Theo.

THEO *(smiles)* Dear Maudie.

MAUD ALLAN I practice day and night, and otherwise think only of you. I will make you proud of me, my darling Theo.

THEO I am proud of you.

MAUD ALLAN Oh Theo, I know you are innocent; why can't we prove it? Why are we so persecuted?

THEO Fear nothing, dearest sister, all will be well.

MAUD ALLAN I will write a letter to the governor, begging him to spare you.

THEO Maudie.

MAUD ALLAN I will write it as a grief stricken sister on behalf of my precious brother to ask that you: Governor, esteemed sir, save Theodore Durrant from the terrible fate that hangs over him. If only you could take one look into his past life, before the contemptible press sent their lies like a fog to obliterate his true nature from public sight. You too would see the noble boy that I do. I kneel before you from across the sea and pray that my words reach your heart.

THEO Maud.

MAUD ALLAN And I'll sign it, Theo, I'll sign it humbly, that I am, with the deepest regard for your judgement and decision, yours in sorrow and affliction, Maud Durrant.

THEO Maudie.

MAUD ALLAN And he will pardon you!

THEO Nothing can be done now, Maudie.

MAUD ALLAN That's not true.

THEO I am wearing the locket you gave to me on the day you left, the one with your picture inside. I feel you against my heart, and we are together again. …There is within us a mystery, deep and intricate, which I believe someday will be understood. …Some people still think I can clear one mystery, if only I would say I am guilty. But, it is a mistake to lie in the moment before one is to meet with God. A dishonoring stain on one's name is worse than death.

MAUD ALLAN So it is true, that you didn't do it. You didn't do it, did you, Theo.

THEO …It rained all last night. The first rain of winter. The farmers will be glad. But now it is quiet, and looks as though it may clear up. I feel myself high above ordinary things, and trouble seems to have been lifted from my soul. Oh I wish that you could feel the lightness that I feel now. My dear sister. I have missed you so. Your music. Your beautiful face. Your embrace. Why did you leave me when you did?

> *MAUD covers her face with her hands. THIRD GUARD puts away his watch and steps forward. THEO notices.*

THEO …And now, with much love, I will bring this to a close. Au revoir for a time. Affectionately, and always. Theo.

MAUD ALLAN "Theo."

ISABELLA DURRANT My Theo.

THIRD GUARD Do you wish to say anything?

> *THEO looks at THIRD GUARD, and then out across the audience. His tone is calm but pointed.*

THEO …Do you wish me to say anything? What do you wish me to say? Well I would like to say this. That I hold no animosity toward those authorities who persecuted me, nor the press who hounded me to the grave. I forgive them all. They will receive their justice from God, to whom I now go to receive mine. This city, this country, and this world will be forever blackened with the crime of my innocent blood. My hands are free from all stains that would be painted upon them. I am innocent of the crimes charged against me. That is what I wish to say. I am innocent. I am innocent. I am innoce–

> *The floor drops out from under THEO and he falls suddenly with a crash and dies at the end of the tight rope. A guttural gasp escapes from ISABELLA.*
>
> *With great difficulty ISABELLA pulls herself up and together. There is an iciness about her now.*

ISABELLA DURRANT ...Dearest Maud.

MAUD ALLAN Why was I not home to be with him? He would not have missed me! He would not have taken it out on those girls!

ISABELLA DURRANT *(warning)* Darling.

MAUD ALLAN If only I had not come to Germany! None of this would have happened!

ISABELLA DURRANT Daughter! ...Do not lose your courage.

MAUD ALLAN Have I?

ISABELLA DURRANT You must not.

MAUD ALLAN No.

ISABELLA DURRANT It is actually the most fortunate stroke of luck that you have been away, my darling. The land and sea that divides us protects your own right to fame from your brother's wrongful infamy. You have an opportunity that you must not overlook, for in it lies your success, and the future of our family's name. And it would break your dear brother's heart if you let anything stop you. Your grief will lend your music a charm that cannot be taught.

MAUD ALLAN I can't play music now!

ISABELLA DURRANT You must–

MAUD ALLAN Drilling like a soldier in this cage of notes and measures? I can't–!

ISABELLA DURRANT –You must: find a way. You will always be your brother's sister. But you must make a name for yourself.

MAUD ALLAN I must.

ISABELLA DURRANT Nothing else now can make up for our loss but showing the world that you are, as he was, ambitious.

> *Music. MAUD moves involuntarily. Then, with each line, MAUD moves like a jolt, and then increasingly like a dance, as if each thing she says is*

gradually yanking the dance out of her.

MAUD ALLAN I must– ...I must–
ISABELLA DURRANT So: take your father's name as your last.
MAUD ALLAN Maud Allan.
ISABELLA DURRANT Make it the only name you have.
MAUD ALLAN It is the only name I have.
ISABELLA DURRANT That you may be your own sensation.
MAUD ALLAN Miss Maud Allan.
ISABELLA DURRANT Do it now, my dear. Close your teeth and say: I will.
MAUD ALLAN No matter what happens.
ISABELLA DURRANT I will.
MAUD ALLAN No matter what has happened.
ISABELLA DURRANT I will.
MAUD ALLAN God help me!
ISABELLA DURRANT Or die in the attempt.
MAUD ALLAN I will!

MAUD's dance takes off, becoming evermore ecstatic and impassioned. Over the course of it she sheds her proper dress and emerges as the vision of Salome for which she became famous. Suddenly it ends and huge applause erupts. MAUD stands dazed, taking it in as bouquets of red poppies drop from the sky around her, and:

THEO Maudie?
ISABELLA DURRANT Maud Darling?
JUDGE DARLING Miss Durrant!
HUME-WILLIAMS Miss Allan!
SECOND GUARD Maud Allan?
BILLING Maud Allan Durrant!

At the sound of JUDGE DARLING'S gavel, the applause goes silent.

JUDGE DARLING Ladies and gentleman, the Court is adjourned until after intermission.

TITLE: "Intermission"

Intermission

Scene Six

> *Distant gunfire and shells can be heard. They seem to be growing steadily closer. MAUD enters slowly, listening intently, and still dressed in her "Vision of Salome" costume, which she wears continually from now on.*
>
> *Suddenly the shelling is upon us. The SIX BRITISH SOLDIERS fly over the top of the trench and slide down into the mud below. The explosions cease. THE SOLDIERS catch their breath solemnly in the wake of it.*
>
> *Lazy piano music – maybe Satie. THE SOLDIERS go about their business, starting by routinely removing their bayonets from the ends of their rifles, and from there...*
>
> *...We are in a pub, late at night. There is a BARTENDER. Near him at the bar is a BUSINESS MAN, drinking a pint. SARA, a young woman, is seated alone at a table, drinking a pint. SOLDIERS ONE and THREE sit in the trench preoccupied with their own thoughts, not drinking, though they could just as likely be in the lonely pub as well by their distant looks.*
>
> *MAUD stalks about, unseen by the others, sometimes in her own thoughts, mostly observing various of them in particular – listening, watching, an antenna and receiver for others' emotions, her movements subtle, careful and deliberate. (She will continue to be a presence in this fashion throughout the remainder of the play, even in the court scenes.)*
>
> *SOLDIER SIX enters the pub. SARA notices him.*

BARTENDER Oi.
SOLDIER SIX A pint?

> TITLE: "A small pub in London, late at night."
>
> *BARTENDER obliges. SOLDIER SIX tries to pay.*

BARTENDER Nah.
SOLDIER SIX Cheers.
BUSINESS MAN Good show, old boy.

> *BUSINESS MAN claps SOLDIER SIX on the back with a show of sincerity. SOLDIER SIX smiles and moves away, stands alone to savor*

the first quaff of his pint.

SARA You alone?

SOLDIER SIX Are you?

SARA Yeh. For now. Sit yerself?

SOLDIER SIX does.

SARA I'm Sara. You on leave?

SOLDIER SIX Yeh.

SARA How long?

SOLDIER SIX Two days.

SARA What's today?

SOLDIER SIX Day one.

SARA Having a good time?

SOLDIER SIX *(smiles wearily)* ...Yeh.

SARA Not very convincing.

SOLDIER SIX I wouldn't make a very good actor, would I?

SARA Would you want to be?

SOLDIER SIX What?

SARA Be an actor?

SOLDIER SIX No. Might feel redundant.

SARA What?

SOLDIER SIX ...What do you want to be?

SARA Having a good time.

SOLDIER SIX And you picked this pub?

SARA Yeh. It's quiet. Not like most London pubs. What did you do with day one?

SOLDIER SIX Went to the circus.

SARA Circus? Where?

SOLDIER SIX Down at the Old Baily.

SARA There's a circus near there?

SOLDIER SIX The Maud Allan Billing trial.

SARA *(impressed)* You saw that? How'd you get a seat? I hear it's mad.

SOLDIER SIX They were putting wounded soldiers in the gallery. Brought them in to cheer Billing on, I think. I just slipped in with the rest.

SARA Are you wounded?

SOLDIER SIX Not yet.

SARA ...What's it like?

SOLDIER SIX Getting wounded?

SARA No, silly, the trial.

SOLDIER SIX Billing is the ring master. Judge Darling is the clown. Maud Allan is the girl on the flying trapeze. And everyone watches with baited breath, waiting to see if she'll fall. I half suspect they'd prefer it. That's why we go to the circus, right? The possibility we might see someone fall?

SARA Never thought about it like that. I just thought it was a bit of fun.

SOLDIER SIX The trial?

SARA The circus. ...What was Maud Allan wearing?

SOLDIER SIX Oh, something.

SARA I'd like to be famous. Wear something. Go to posh dinner parties. Social events.

SOLDIER SIX Court.

SARA ...I think you could use a bit of fun. Maybe you should have gone to an actual circus.

SOLDIER SIX I went to the theatre.

SARA Tonight?

SOLDIER SIX After the trial.

SARA Cor, you must be knackered.

SOLDIER SIX Breakfast in France. Lunch in London. Afternoon at the Old Baily. Evening at the theatre. A pint with Sara.

THEY clink pints.

SOLDIER SIX It's absurd when you think about it.

SARA What is?

SOLDIER SIX The juxtaposition.

SARA The what?

SOLDIER SIX ...Why are you here all by yerself? A young lady.

SARA I have me reasons. Besides, why shouldn't I do what I like?

SOLDIER SIX You're not married?

SARA I was.

SOLDIER SIX A soldier?

SARA Yeh, and a brute before that. When he joined the ranks, peace broke out. The only peace I ever 'ad. When I got word the Kaiser had taken him I thought good, the Kaiser can bloody 'ave him. I'm going to have me a bleedin' good time from now on.

SOLDIER SIX Do you?

SARA I do alright. Work in the munitions factory, pays a living. Stay with me Mum, she cooks, glad to have me back. Lets me do as I please.

SOLDIER SIX And your Dad?

SARA Kaiser took him too. It's not sad, though. I learned to pick a husband from me Mum. She'd be in the pub now herself if she didn't still believe in Sundays. "Jesus is the only man what never let me down," she says. ...Oh, I'm sorry.

SOLDIER SIX What for?

SARA You're a soldier and here I am thanking the bloody Kaiser. That's no consolation, is it?

SOLDIER SIX 'S alright. The only real consolation I get from coming home is that every time I do the women's skirts are a bit shorter.

SARA Ha! You're a dirty bugger. ...Me Mum still cries about me Dad, even though he was a bastard. ...Everyone says we need to show you men on leave a good time. Help you forget what you've got to go back to.

SOLDIER SIX I don't want to forget. I have to remember, since nobody here intends to. That trial today. Everyone in their finery. And the soldiers in the gallery like sideshow freaks to the main act. At the theatre tonight all I could think about was the trench. Sunset over No Man's Land is a most theatrical moment. The lights go down. You can almost hear the orchestra tuning up and the last thumps behind the curtain. It's exciting. Waiting to run into Jerry's fire has that feeling I remember coming over me when I was a kid performing in amateur theatricals before the curtain went up. There we are, ready in the wings. And across the stage an audience is waiting in the dark to give us the reception we deserve.

SARA ...You don't deserve it. I can tell. You're not like me husband or me dad.

SOLDIER SIX No?

SARA You think too much.

SOLDIER SIX Dirty thoughts sometimes.

SARA Yeh? What about?

SOLDIER SIX You.

SARA What were you thinkin' about me?

SOLDIER SIX Your lips. Your breasts. Your soft navel. The gentle slope of your belly. Your tuft of hair. My hands beneath your bum, lifting your pelvis to my mouth. And me drinking from you like a cup of red wine, learning you with my tongue.

SARA ...Cor. Is that what you were thinkin'? ...What else?

SOLDIER SIX ...You really want to know?

SARA Yeh.

SOLDIER SIX That gent over there.

SARA You're thinkin' about him?

SOLDIER SIX How I'd like a tank to crash through this pub and flatten him.

SARA Blighmy! What for?

SOLDIER SIX What did he do to enjoy a pint? He's a pub general, I'd wager. Drinks beer and pisses strategic advice. You know what I heard one like him say at intermission tonight? "Lost heavily in that last scrap." You don't talk like that if you've watched men die. I loathe these business men. I hate smiling women in the streets. I hope the politicians die by poison-gas. I pray God to get the Germans to send Zeppelins to England – make the people know what it means. ...Those are my dirty thoughts. You have any?

SARA ...I like air raids. ...It's a terrible thing to say, isn't it. All that damage. People killed. But every time the siren goes, I feel this big rush of exhilaration. I'd really like to go out and run about in it! I don't of course. But I get this feeling that the surface of everything is starting to crack. Do you ever feel that?

SOLDIER SIX ...I don't know what to make of you. I've gotten out of touch with women. They seem to have changed so much, expanded in all directions, while us men have been shrunk down and stuffed in ditches.

SARA I just want to enjoy this peace while I can. I'm afraid about what will happen when the war ends.

SOLDIER SIX I envy you. I despise you. I am quite determined to get you. You owe me something, all of you do. And they can all pay through you.

SARA ...I'll pay.

> ...After a moment, SARA stands up and offers SOLDIER SIX her hand. HE doesn't move. SARA sits back down. SOLDIER SIX stands up as if to leave, and SARA quickly but carefully stands up with him. ...But then SOLDIER SIX steps closer to SARA and they begin to slow dance to the music. MAUD dances what's inside of them both, swaying gently beside them as they do. SOLDIER THREE dances with an imaginary partner, incidentally dancing as the woman.
>
> The BUSINESS MAN laughs over naughty small talk with the patient BARTENDER. SOLDIER SIX looks at them. SARA pulls his attention back to her and kisses him.
>
> SARA pulls away gently and looks troubled.

SARA ...I abandoned him.

SOLDIER SIX Who?

SARA Me husband.

> MAUD watches SARA.

SOLDIER SIX I thought he was a brute.

SARA He was. I wasn't there for him when he died. I've thought terrible things. I feel so bad... I guess I'll always be me Mum's daughter.

SOLDIER SIX ...Would you like to go? I'm not pushing, but if you wanted to, I'd make sure it went alright.

SARA I trust you.

> *This troubles SOLDIER SIX. He stares at SARA. MAUD stares at SOLDIER SIX. In fact, EVERYONE is now watching SARA and SOLDIER SIX. SOLDIER SIX touches SARA'S hair.*

Scene Seven

> *Shift. JUDGE DARLING takes his seat in court. SECOND GUARD takes up his position. As SECOND GUARD gets things going, BILLING very quickly checks in with EILEEN for some quite last minute notes prior to going on for this, his second act.*

SECOND GUARD Please come to order.

> TITLE: "30 May, 1918. Day Two in the trial of Maud Allan v. Noel Pemberton-Billing at the Old Baily Central Criminal Court."

SECOND GUARD The court is now back in session. The honorable Sir Justice Darling presiding.

JUDGE DARLING Thank you, ladies and gentlemen. Gentlemen of the jury. And welcome back to the case of Maud Allan versus Noel Pemberton-Billing. Mr. Billing, you may introduce your next witness:

> *BILLING has escorted EILEEN to the witness box.*

BILLING Thank you, My Lord; I will now call Mrs. Eileen Villiers-Stuart.

JUDGE DARLING Proceed.

BILLING Mrs. Villiers-Stuart, have you read the alleged libel figuring in this case?

EILEEN VILLIERS-STUART I have.

BILLING Have you also read the *Vigilante* article on the subject of a German Black Book containing the names of forty-seven thousand traitors to this country, acting in the service of Germany.

EILEEN VILLIERS-STUART I have read the article, yes.

BILLING Have you seen that book yourself in this country?

EILEEN VILLIERS-STUART I have.

BILLING And are the statements made about that book in the *Vigilante* article true in substance and in fact?

EILEEN VILLIERS-STUART Absolutely.

HUME-WILLIAMS My Lord, no evidence has been given of the existence of this book.

JUDGE DARLING Mr. Billing, do you intend to produce this book?

BILLING Not at the moment, my Lord.

JUDGE DARLING What do you mean not at the moment? Is it in this Court or is it not?

BILLING It is not.

JUDGE DARLING Do you know where it is?

BILLING The evidence you will have put before you, I think, will answer that question.

JUDGE DARLING Mrs. Villiers-Stuart, you will leave the witness box.

BILLING My Lord / Justice Darling!

JUDGE DARLING I shall not allow evidence to be given of a document which ought to be produced.

BILLING It will be impossible to produce the book at this stage of this trial.

JUDGE DARLING It is no use to tell me that it will be impossible to produce it. You must tell me where it is. If you cannot get it, perhaps I can. I still have some powers left.

Laughter in court.

BILLING My Lord, such information will be revealed, if this examination is allowed to proceed, that proves the book does in fact exist.

JUDGE DARLING Very well.

BILLING Now. Mrs. Villiers-Stuart. You say that you have actually seen and handled that book.

EILEEN VILLIERS-STUART I have seen it and I have handled it.

BILLING You would recognize it if you saw it again?

EILEEN VILLIERS-STUART Instantly.

BILLING Who showed you the book?

EILEEN VILLIERS-STUART ...Is that question quite necessary to answer?

JUDGE DARLING Answer that question.

EILEEN VILLIERS-STUART ...Neil Primrose.

BILLING The former Chief Whip of Herbert Asquith.

EILEEN VILLIERS-STUART Yes.

BILLING Where exactly were you when Neil Primrose showed you the book?

EILEEN VILLIERS-STUART ...In Ripley. He showed it to me – over tea – at, a small hotel there.

BILLING Was anyone else present beside Mr. Primrose?

EILEEN VILLIERS-STUART No.

BILLING And where is Mr. Primrose now?

EILEEN VILLIERS-STUART He was killed in Palestine.

BILLING He is unfortunately dead?

EILEEN VILLIERS-STUART Yes. Because he knew of the book!

JUDGE DARLING You say Neil Primrose, Chief Whip to Herbert Asquith, was killed in Palestine not in the line of duty but because he knew of this book?

EILEEN VILLIERS-STUART I say so, yes.

JUDGE DARLING Are you sure you wish to suggest such a thing, Mrs. Villiers-Stuart?

EILEEN VILLIERS-STUART It is not a suggestion, it is the truth.

JUDGE DARLING You will have to help your witness prove this, Mr. Billing.

BILLING Mrs. Villiers-Stuart, did you see the names listed in the book?

HUME-WILLIAMS My Lord.

JUDGE DARLING I have told you, Mr. Billing, you must prove a great deal more before you can give evidence of that book's contents.

BILLING ...Why did you come forward to give evidence in this case?

JUDGE DARLING It is entirely immaterial why she came forward.

BILLING ...Are you acquainted with the fact that there exists, in this country / a–

JUDGE DARLING You must not put a leading question.

BILLING Are the claims made in the Vigilante article true that that book contains the names of corruptible British Cabinet Ministers, wives / of Cabinet Ministers, newspaper editors, diplomats, bankers, even members of His Majesty's own household?

JUDGE DARLING Oh, / dear god. Mr. Billing!

HUME-WILLIAMS I object!

EILEEN VILLIERS-STUART It is absolutely true!

JUDGE DARLING You have no right to ask that question. To do so you must produce the book.

BILLING The last known holder of the book is dead, my Lord. I cannot call him to produce the book.

JUDGE DARLING Then you must call someone else. I have allowed you a great deal of latitude, Mr. Billing, but if you are to conduct your own case you must conduct it according to the ordinary rules of law.

BILLING I know nothing about law! I come to this Court in the public interest to prove what I must prove!

JUDGE DARLING Very well, then you must prove it according to the rules of law.

BILLING My Lord, I say this–

JUDGE DARLING –I do not wish you to say anything to me! I only ask you not to put leading questions to your witness!

BILLING ...Is Justice Darling's name in that book?

JUDGE DARLING Ah!

EILEEN VILLIERS-STUART It is!

JUDGE DARLING Just one moment!

BILLING Is Herbert Asquith's name in that book?

EILEEN VILLIERS-STUART It is!

BILLING Is Margot Asquith's name in that book?

EILEEN VILLIERS-STUART It is!

JUDGE DARLING You will be silent!

EILEEN VILLIERS-STUART And that book can be produced!

JUDGE DARLING It can be produced?!

EILEEN VILLIERS-STUART Mr. Justice Darling, we have got to win this war, and while you sit there we will never win it! Our men are fighting! Our men are dying!

JUDGE DARLING You will leave the witness box this instant!

EILEEN VILLIERS-STUART You dare not dismiss me!

JUDGE DARLING Have you quite finished asking questions of this character?

BILLING I have not, my Lord!

JUDGE DARLING Then I tell you to sit down!

BILLING My Lord, it will take more than you to protect the names listed in that book.

JUDGE DARLING If you do not conduct yourself properly there will very soon be an end to this case altogether.

EILEEN VILLIERS-STUART If you are convicted, Mr. Billing, I will carry on!

JUDGE DARLING Do not interfere. You say this book can be produced?

EILEEN VILLIERS-STUART It can be produced and it will be produced and when it is every name inside of it will be revealed! Every name, Lord Justice Darling, do you hear me?

A tense moment.

JUDGE DARLING ...You will resume your examination please, and remember

what I have said.
BILLING Do you propose to go on trying this case, my Lord?
JUDGE DARLING Resume your examination.
BILLING What other names are listed in that book?
JUDGE DARLING Mr. Billing!

Scene Eight

> *Shift. BILLING, SPENCER and EILEEN in Billing's office later that night. BILLING laughs; HE is in a good mood.*

EILEEN VILLIERS-STUART You promised me!

> TITLE: "Billing's office, later that night."

EILEEN VILLIERS-STUART You promised that you would not ask me to name names!
BILLING It had to be done.
EILEEN VILLIERS-STUART But you promised!
BILLING *(pleased)* And you named names!
EILEEN VILLIERS-STUART Once you had begun I couldn't very well go against you.
BILLING It's good that you didn't.
EILEEN VILLIERS-STUART Noel, I was with Neil Primrose at that hotel in Ripley because we were having an affair! If that comes out I shall be discredited entirely!
BILLING You had an affair with Neil Primrose?
EILEEN VILLIERS-STUART Yes!
BILLING You should have told me that.
SPENCER Anyway, the Black Book is now on the table, that's the main thing. And I'll be there tomorrow to support your evidence.
EILEEN VILLIERS-STUART You will? How?
SPENCER I'll say that I saw the book, –
EILEEN VILLIERS-STUART Have you?
SPENCER Yes, and that Neil Primrose showed it to me.
EILEEN VILLIERS-STUART Did he?
SPENCER No, but–
EILEEN VILLIERS-STUART –And you're going to allow him to tell this lie in Court?

BILLING He will have to tell it, in order to corroborate your evidence, because if he does not, they may not believe you.

EILEEN VILLIERS-STUART But he'll be lying.

BILLING Yes, I know. But it's got to be done. Although, best not to keep Primrose in the mix, under the circumstances *(i.e. Eileen's affair with him)*, eh Spencer?

SPENCER Right. Hume-Williams won't ask after Primrose either. It wouldn't do him good to emphasize that Asquith's Chief Whip was harboring a copy of the Black Book, now would it?

BILLING No.

EILEEN VILLIERS-STUART The book exists. Its threats are real. We don't need to tell lies to prove it. If we do and it comes out, a major German conspiracy against this country will continue to be ignored.

BILLING Can you produce the book?

EILEEN VILLIERS-STUART No!

BILLING Neither can I. And you're right, this threat must no longer be ignored. So here we are.

SPENCER The German Prince showed the book to me personally. We'll keep it to that.

BILLING Yes.

EILEEN VILLIERS-STUART Noel. There's something else. When I left the Court today a man handed me a letter threatening my life unless I return to the service of my employers and do all that I can to secure your downfall.

BILLING Who was the man?

EILEEN VILLIERS-STUART I didn't know him.

BILLING Who wrote the letter?

EILEEN VILLIERS-STUART There was no signature! Who would sign such a thing?

SPENCER Obviously it was from Asquith and Lloyd George's people. Your employers. I told you she was risky.

EILEEN VILLIERS-STUART I should never have mentioned the names. What shall I do?

BILLING Stay one step ahead, of course. We'll draft a statement for you to sign, verifying your testimony, your employment by them to entrap me, and now this death threat.

EILEEN VILLIERS-STUART In writing? Why should we do that?

BILLING If something were to happen to you we'd need it.

EILEEN VILLIERS-STUART ...Noel!

BILLING Pemberton-Billing.

Scene Nine

JUDGE DARLING Mr. Billing?

Shift.

JUDGE DARLING You may call your next witness.

TITLE: "31 May, 1918. Day Three of the trial."

BILLING Thank you, my Lord. I will now call Captain Harold Spencer.

SPENCER takes his place in the witness box. EILEEN soon leaves, stunned.

BILLING Captain Spencer, what is your history with the British Secret Service?

SPENCER In 1913 I was a member of the International Commission to Albania, where I became aide-de-camp to the king of Albania, the German prince William of Wied. When fighting broke out there in 1914 I left for Italy, about mid-September. But during my time with the Prince I had access to his private papers and obtained a great deal of information.

BILLING Touching on what?

SPENCER I was principally interested in what action was to be taken by Germany in the event of war with England. The Prince's papers fully explained this, and I reported these things to the British Foreign Office.

BILLING Did you report the incident of your having discovered the Black Book referred to in the *Vigilante* article?

HUME-WILLIAMS My Lord, Captain Spencer has not said that he discovered the book.

BILLING I will go back.

JUDGE DARLING Probably it will save a good deal of time if he just answers the question.

HUME-WILLIAMS My Lord–!

JUDGE DARLING Psht. Captain Spencer.

SPENCER I did report the book, to the private secretaries of Mr. Herbert Asquith, that it had been shown to me by the Prince personally, and that it contained a list compiled by German agents of the names of people in England who might be coerced for information.

BILLING And when you reported the book to the private secretaries of Mr. Herbert Asquith, what was their response?

SPENCER They told me it would undermine the whole fabric of the British Government if it was made public, that the book was not here in Downing

Street so let the matter go. It was insinuated that I might disappear with it if it did not. That's when I realized the whole thing was hopeless, that the Germans had such a grip on our affairs that nothing could be done, and I came to work for you at *The Vigilante*. If the government wouldn't help England I hoped journalism might, and to hell with those who might try anything to stop us from breaking the grip of German agents murdering our men in France. Let them threaten my life if they like!

Applause in court.

Shift. MAUD now speaks, though the court takes no note of her. (Throughout this scene we seem to slip between reality and Maud's unnoticed observations of it as she "writes" her letter to her mother.)

MAUD ALLAN Dearest Mama. I am sorry this reply to your recent letter comes so late. In brief: no, I do not think now would be a good time for you to visit me here in London. I shall spare you the worst of the details. But I will tell you that, although I am the plaintiff in this case, I feel very much the defendant in some other case all together. Sitting in this court, I find myself now a forgotten page in my own story, which has been written over entirely by Mr. Billing's grim fairy tale. You would be appalled by what this man deems fit to say.

BILLING Let us turn now to that paragraph which constitutes the alleged libel. You, Captain Spencer, in fact, drafted this paragraph, did you not?

SPENCER I did.

BILLING How did you come about the title?

MAUD ALLAN I find myself often wondering how much even he understands of what he says.

SPENCER I tried to find a title that would only be understood by those whom it should be understood by.

BILLING And to that end you consulted the village doctor?

SPENCER I did, and he provided me with a certain anatomical name.

BILLING What was the name?

SPENCER Clitoris.

JUDGE DARLING Ah. The Greek chap. Finally.

BILLING Captain Spencer, could you share with us the meaning of this name?

MAUD ALLAN What any of these men understand about their poor, unfortunate wives one can only guess.

SPENCER According to the doctor, the clitoris is a superficial organ that, when unduly excited or over-developed, possesses the most dreadful influence on any woman, such that she would do the most extraordinary things if she was over-stimulated in a superficial manner.

BILLING And why did you think it imperative to print the title and content of the alleged libel?

SPENCER In order to help draw attention to what the Black Book indicated their methods of corruption were.

BILLING And what did the book indicate in regard to their methods?

MAUD ALLAN It strikes me that these men are too distracted by their own fantasies to be bothered with understanding those of a woman.

SPENCER Sodomy. Lesbianism. Both of which are unnatural vices and one a criminal offense.

BILLING And the German agents practice these vices to bring into bondage English people?

SPENCER That is their objective, yes. Should people succumb, the fact is then held over them as blackmail, and they must do whatever their superiors want.

MAUD ALLAN They would seem to think anyone with a healthy desire to live life according to the heart's liberty, would readily lend her name to their little Black Book's ledger, and her body to the destruction of the world as they know it.

BILLING provides SPENCER with a copy of Salome.

BILLING Captain Spencer, have you read this play, *Salome*, by Oscar Wilde?

MAUD ALLAN Whether she is real or imagined.

SPENCER I have.

BILLING What vices do you find illustrated in this play that caused you to employ the expression, "The Cult of the Clitoris"?

SPENCER Sadism, mainly.

BILLING Can you offer an example?

SPENCER Yes. Toward the end.

JUDGE DARLING Ope. What page?

SPENCER Sixty-three.

JUDGE DARLING Thank you.

SPENCER Salome is holding the decapitated head of John the Baptist, and she says, "Thou wouldst not suffer me to kiss thy mouth, Iokanaan. Well! I will kiss it now. I will bite it with my teeth as one bites a ripe fruit." That is pure sadism. And it goes on: "Yes, I will kiss thy mouth, Iokanaan. I said it. Did I not say it? I said it, I will kiss it now!" It is the mutterings of a child suffering from an enlarged and diseased clitoris.

HUME-WILLIAMS bursts out laughing, and as he tries to control it:

HUME-WILLIAMS *(to DARLING:)* I'm sorry. Sorry.

BILLING I beg to call your Lordship's attention to the humor that this arouses in Counsel.

SPENCER I think the Germans were very clever in advocating this play as a means of corrupting people with sadism.

JUDGE DARLING You were not asked what you think about the Germans.

SPENCER My Lord, when the country is at stake and soldiers are dying in France–

JUDGE DARLING –That is nonsense.

SPENCER It is not nonsense, it is the question of today!

JUDGE DARLING The question of today is whether this paragraph is a libel or not! You are not here to address the Court about soldiers in France.

SPENCER Someone must speak for them!

Applause in court.

BILLING *(with flourish)* I submit this witness for cross examination!

JUDGE DARLING No you do not! He will be cross-examined as a matter of course without your introduction. He is not an actor whom you present to an audience. Now sit! Mr. Hume-Williams, if you please!

HUME-WILLIAMS Thank you, my Lord.

MAUD ALLAN But I have faith, Mama, that my counsel, Mr. Hume-Williams, will trip up these spiders in their own absurd webs.

HUME-WILLIAMS Captain Spencer.

MAUD ALLAN The most effective webs being, invariably, one's own.

HUME-WILLIAMS You explained to the court a moment ago that the clitoris is part of the female organ.

SPENCER A superficial part.

HUME-WILLIAMS In which the sexual sensations are produced?

SPENCER It is what remains of the male organ in the female.

HUME-WILLIAMS And when stimulated it effects a woman's behavior improperly, you say.

SPENCER An exaggerated clitoris might even drive a woman to an elephant.

HUME-WILLIAMS Captain Spencer, do you give as your considered opinion that the actions of the character Salome in Oscar Wilde's play are indeed sadism?

SPENCER And produced an orgasm.

JUDGE DARLING A what?

HUME-WILLIAMS What is the word you used?

SPENCER Orgasm.

HUME-WILLIAMS What is it, some unnatural vice?

MAUD ALLAN Or perhaps I speak too soon in praise of Mister Hume-Williams.

SPENCER As the doctor explained it to me, it is a function of the body. Anyone with perverted instincts would take extreme delight in the play, and, while watching it, probably have an orgasm themselves. Orgasms are of great interest to the Germans.

JUDGE DARLING Germans again! You are not asked about the Germans. Get the Germans out of your head.

SPENCER I wish more people would get them in.

HUME-WILLIAMS I will ask you about your Germans, Captain Spencer.

SPENCER They are not my Germans.

HUME-WILLIAMS You obtained this information about the Black Book from your German prince in Albania while in secret service to your country, correct?

SPENCER He was not my prince and my service was no secret to my country, to my employers that is.

HUME-WILLIAMS Your employers, the British Secret Service, knew everything you were doing?

SPENCER I reported everything to them; they did nothing with it, as I've said.

HUME-WILLIAMS Would you say these reports were of a very sensitive nature?

SPENCER Very sensitive.

HUME-WILLIAMS And those sensitive reports are the property of your employers, of the Government.

SPENCER They are the property of the country.

HUME-WILLIAMS And as a Government servant to this country are you at liberty to publish sensitive reports of this kind to the world?

SPENCER Not as a rule.

HUME-WILLIAMS So, then, when you published your information about the Black Book and the first forty-seven thousand, did you first obtain permission from the Government to break this rule?

SPENCER I sent copies of the article to everyone after it was written.

HUME-WILLIAMS Well! It does not do much good after the fact, does it?

SPENCER It has done a great deal of good.

HUME-WILLIAMS So it is good policy, you say, to break the rules of your service to this country first, and tell people afterwards?

SPENCER It was my duty.

HUME-WILLIAMS To your employers.

SPENCER To my country.

HUME-WILLIAMS If it is a rule of service to this country not to make sensitive information public, how can it be your duty to break it?

SPENCER Because the circumstances of this war are such that some rules must be broken to win!

> *This goes down well in Court.*

HUME-WILLIAMS ...Captain Spencer, what is your nationality?

SPENCER I was born by the English Great Lakes, in Wisconsin. I was technically born on the British Canadian border.

HUME-WILLIAMS Were you born an American subject, or British?

SPENCER I could claim American nationality.

HUME-WILLIAMS Do you?

MAUD ALLAN This Mister Spencer is beginning to feel as I have the pressure of what it is to be foreign in a time of fear.

JUDGE DARLING Answer the question.

MAUD ALLAN The locals do not forget,

SPENCER I have never been naturalized British.

MAUD ALLAN or forgive.

HUME-WILLIAMS So your duty in this instance is not to your country, but to your British employers.

JUDGE DARLING ...Captain Spencer?

SPENCER That was a question?

HUME-WILLIAMS It was.

SPENCER To my British employers, yes.

HUME-WILLIAMS And you betrayed them.

SPENCER No.

HUME-WILLIAMS You broke the rules.

SPENCER I have said why. It was necessary. And if more people in England showed such initiative this war would have been won long ago and America's help would not have been necessary.

> *This does not go down well in Court.*

MAUD ALLAN As this trial presses on around me, despite me, in my neglected corner of this madhouse I sometimes feel close to madness myself, and long to either break certain heads or else break out and run freely in the streets. I trust it won't be long now. Mr. Hume-Williams seems to be jangling the right keys closer to the door.

HUME-WILLIAMS After your time in Albania you say you spent time in Italy. What were you doing there?

SPENCER I had been transferred to the British Embassy there to continue my service.

HUME-WILLIAMS And it was there that you were invalided out of service, correct?

SPENCER ...Correct.

HUME-WILLIAMS In what way, invalided? ...Captain Spencer?

SPENCER I was declared medically unfit.

HUME-WILLIAMS In what way, medically unfit?

SPENCER ...It was suggested by my superiors that I was suffering from hallucinations.

HUME-WILLIAMS Hallucinations! With regard to what?

SPENCER They said, with regard to my reports about German agents and the book. It was the easiest way to shut me up. It is often done in the Secret Service. People are shut up, declared ins– er, mentally– medically unfit, or get marooned on islands.

HUME-WILLIAMS This is an English system?

SPENCER It is a German system practiced in England under the influence of German agents.

HUME-WILLIAMS One moment: You are saying that there are Germans in England holding such important positions that they are able to get British Secret Service agents declared insane and marooned on islands?

SPENCER Yes!

HUME-WILLIAMS And how do you propose such people get appointed?

SPENCER By the Crown.

This creates a stir in the court.

HUME-WILLIAMS By the Crown, you say!

SPENCER Just look at the action the Crown has seen fit to take against Mr. Billing because I did not keep silent about certain things and he published them in his newspaper.

HUME-WILLIAMS Are you suggesting that this Prosecution has been brought about by anyone other than Miss Allan? That it has some origin in politics?

SPENCER You would know much more about that than I. But it stands to reason. Why else would a civil libel case of this kind, brought about to clear some dancer's name, be tried in a Criminal court, where the defendant can be quite conveniently locked away and thrown out of sight?

HUME-WILLIAMS Captain Spencer–

SPENCER –Answer my question, Mr. Hume-Williams! Or better yet, ask it of your client, Maud Allan! Or is Herbert Asquith your client?

JUDGE DARLING Captain Spencer!

SPENCER Who is your client, Mr. Hume-Williams?!

JUDGE DARLING Captain Spencer!

Scene Ten

Shift.

SPENCER Billing, that was dangerous.

TITLE: "Billing's office, later that night."

BILLING I was there, Spencer.

SPENCER If they can get me written off as insane the Black Book could be entirely dismissed.

BILLING You might have told me the reason you were invalided out of service, Spencer. I'd assumed you had been wounded, that it was a war hero I'd hired and was now calling into the witness box!

SPENCER Get off it, Billing. Why would I go about advertising my having been declared mentally unstable. It isn't true. Anyway our problem stands.

BILLING I can't see how to proceed with the Black Book without discussing the Black Book. Eileen's further testimony is no longer viable. If now yours isn't either, who do we have?

SPENCER Perhaps we should drop the book altogether.

BILLING Drop it all together? Why did I subject myself to this public trial?

SPENCER Why have / I?

BILLING Why are we here if not to prove the Black Book exists, that a systematic conspiracy is at work to bring England down?

SPENCER As Hume-Williams and Judge Darling are so good to point out repeatedly, we are here in response to Maud Allan's charge of libel.

BILLING This trial is not about Maud Allan; it is about this country winning or losing this war. In the end who cares one jot about Maud Allan!

SPENCER Everyone picking up every newspaper every day, that is who. It's because of her name that finally we have the entire country's attention/.

BILLING –And we cannot squander that!

SPENCER Billing, all I have worked for, since the day I was "invalided out of duty," has been to prove to the British people what their government really is!

Do you think for a moment that I don't understand what this trial is about? ...Now, we began with Maud Allan's character and that of her kind. We threw light on the perverted lot of them and their role in this conspiracy and all Great Britain took notice. If we can't testify any further about the Black Book, let's put the spotlight back on the moral perverts, keep the popular fervor, and end it that way.

BILLING ...You had better be right, Captain.

MAUD ALLAN When this trial is finished, Mama, I will have more to write. God knows what Billing will call forth next. But whatever is to come, may there be some humanity underneath to crack the surface of it. All I have left now is to wait, and to hope.

Scene Eleven

JUDGE DARLING Mr. Billing?

Shift.

MAUD ALLAN Love, your Maudie.

JUDGE DARLING You may call your next witness.

TITLE: "1 June, 1918. Day Four of the trial."

JUDGE DARLING And don't be showy about it.

BILLING ...I call Lord Alfred Douglas.

Accompanied by the same music that underscored MAUD's own Scene Four court entrance, LORD ALFRED DOUGLAS takes the stand as a confident, feline actor might. MAUD takes particular note of him.

JUDGE DARLING What did I say about being showy? ...(brightly:) Good afternoon, Lord Alfred Douglas. I welcome you back to the Old Baily.

LORD ALFRED DOUGLAS *(icily)* Thank you Judge, Darling.

JUDGE DARLING You are most welcome. Mr. Billing.

BILLING Lord Alfred Douglas.

LORD ALFRED DOUGLAS Yes.

BILLING What is your relationship to the play, *Salome*, by Oscar Wilde?

LORD ALFRED DOUGLAS I am its translator, from the original French to English.

BILLING And your relationship to Oscar Wilde himself?

LORD ALFRED DOUGLAS I translated his play.

BILLING In translating his play you must have worked with Mr. Wilde very closely.

LORD ALFRED DOUGLAS To my everlasting regret, yes.

BILLING Do you from your own knowledge know that Oscar Wilde was a sexual and moral pervert?

LORD ALFRED DOUGLAS He admitted to it. He never attempted to disguise it. On the contrary, he gloried in it.

BILLING What in your opinion would be the effect of his play on normally healthy-minded people?

LORD ALFRED DOUGLAS Disgust and revolt, I should think.

BILLING And on sexual perverts?

LORD ALFRED DOUGLAS They would revel in it.

BILLING And those with some taint?

LORD ALFRED DOUGLAS *(eyeing Judge Darling)* On those people it would be liable to awaken any dormant perverse instincts that might lie within them.

BILLING Lord Alfred Douglas, do you know where *Salome* was first produced?

LORD ALFRED DOUGLAS In Berlin. I did not go there see it, of course, but I read something about it.

JUDGE DARLING That will not do.

LORD ALFRED DOUGLAS It is notorious; everyone knows it; it would be ridiculous to deny it.

BILLING Was it a success there?

LORD ALFRED DOUGLAS Quite.

JUDGE DARLING How do you know, if you did not see it?

LORD ALFRED DOUGLAS I read as much, as anyone could have. It's a matter of public record. The play is revived constantly in Germany.

BILLING So it is particularly appealing to the German sensibility?

LORD ALFRED DOUGLAS Indeed. To any – intellectual – sensibility.

BILLING And by "intellectual" do you mean – artistic?

LORD ALFRED DOUGLAS Yes. Whenever Oscar was– Oscar Wilde, was going to do anything particularly revolting, it was always disguised in the most flowery language, and always referred back to Art, in other words to himself. That was his idea of Art. Himself.

BILLING Would you say this self-absorbed attitude of Wilde's toward Art was a Movement of some sort?

LORD ALFRED DOUGLAS Oh yes. Wilde actually spoke of it as The Movement. People were in The Movement for popularizing, and also to free from legal restraint, his particular vice.

BILLING And have they succeeded?

LORD ALFRED DOUGLAS Enormously; if not yet officially.

BILLING Wilde called this a movement. But a more analytical mind would call it a cult?

LORD ALFRED DOUGLAS Yes.

BILLING The Cult of the Clitoris, perhaps?

JUDGE DARLING I do not think we need go into that with him.

BILLING Turning again to the figure of Salome: when Salome declares she wants to touch the body, was it intended by Wilde and yourself to be a carnal or spiritual awakening?

LORD ALFRED DOUGLAS I had nothing to do with it. I merely translated it.

BILLING Did Wilde, then, mean it as a carnal or spiritual awakening?

LORD ALFRED DOUGLAS Carnal. To call it spiritual is a misuse of the word.

BILLING And what about love?

LORD ALFRED DOUGLAS It is absurd to use the word "love" in connection with that play or Wilde in general.

BILLING Would you say Wilde's words, as you translated them, are those of a sodomite?

JUDGE DARLING ...Are they the words of a sodom/ite?

LORD ALFRED DOUGLAS I heard the question thank you Darling. Wilde used words that would be described as "spiritual" only by people like Himself. Those sorts of people always disguise the horribleness of their actions with pretty words. They dare not name the things of which they speak. Not directly, anyway. ...But I have had nothing whatsoever to do with such people for twenty years, so really I cannot be called upon to speak for them.

BILLING Do these people choose to join this movement and adopt this language, or is it hereditary?

LORD ALFRED DOUGLAS It is hereditary.

BILLING That is a fact?

LORD ALFRED DOUGLAS A scientific one.

BILLING Are you aware of the tragedy of Miss Maud Allan's family?

LORD ALFRED DOUGLAS I have heard of it somewhat, yes.

JUDGE DARLING Lord Alfred Douglas.

LORD ALFRED DOUGLAS For god's sake, it was a famous incident written about in public newspapers. One need not have been at the execution personally to know it happened or why.

HUME-WILLIAMS My Lord, once again, what has this matter to do at all with the present case?

BILLING It has everything to do with what I am called upon to prove.

HUME-WILLIAMS It has nothing to do with Miss Allan's present libel.

BILLING Would you agree with that, Lord Alfred Douglas?

JUDGE DARLING It does not matter if he agrees.

LORD ALFRED DOUGLAS I regard Miss Allan as a very unfortunate hereditary degenerate.

JUDGE DARLING You were not asked that.

BILLING Thank you, Lord Alfred Douglas, I have no further questions.

JUDGE DARLING Which means that you, Lord Alfred Douglas, must have no further answers!

LORD ALFRED DOUGLAS I have said what is true.

JUDGE DARLING You have said enough! To my regret, Mr. Hume-Williams must now give you the opportunity to say more. Mr. Hume-Williams, be to the point, if you can.

HUME-WILLIAMS I shall try, my Lord. Lord Alfred Douglas. I understand you to say that Mr. Oscar Wilde had a habit of putting into language of beauty things which, really, were disgusting.

LORD ALFRED DOUGLAS Yes.

HUME-WILLIAMS For instance, is this the sort of thing he would write: "Dearest of all Boys,"

LORD ALFRED DOUGLAS –That is a letter which he wrote to me! It was stolen by that German blackmailer George Lewis, who was my lawyer and who betrayed me and stole that letter and now lends it out for the fiftieth time! Every time I come here, this bestial drivel is brought out! I think there are limits to human endurance!

BILLING Why do they want to drag this muck up?

JUDGE DARLING It is hardly for you to protest against the past muck of a witness being dragged up.

BILLING When a man comes forward and makes a confession in the public interest, it is not right to drag such things up.

JUDGE DARLING If you interrupt again you can leave the Court. What was your question?

HUME-WILLIAMS A letter which the witness says is from Oscar Wilde to himself. It begins, "Dearest of all Boys. You must not make scenes with me. I cannot bare to see your red poppy lips, so Greek and gracious, distorted with passion. You are the divine thing I want, the thing of grace and beauty." Is that a sample of the language you mean?

LORD ALFRED DOUGLAS It is exactly what I said it was: a rotten sodomastically inclined letter written by a diabolical scoundrel to a wretched silly youth. It was first brought out by my father in his effort to smash Wilde

up and save me, and that has been the result. My father went before the Court to save his son, and you lawyers come here twenty-five years later to spit it up again for money. You ought to be ashamed to bring it out here again.
JUDGE DARLING You are not here to comment on Counsel.
LORD ALFRED DOUGLAS You bullied me at my last trial and I shall not be bullied by you again. I shall answer the questions as I please and I shall speak the truth.
JUDGE DARLING You shall not make rude speeches or you will be removed from Court.
LORD ALFRED DOUGLAS Let me be removed from Court! I did not come here to be cross-examined in service to this gang of scoundrel politicians she has backing her!
JUDGE DARLING That is quite enough! Mr. Hume-Williams.
HUME-WILLIAMS When did you cease to approve of sodomy, Lord Alfred Douglas?
LORD ALFRED DOUGLAS When did I–?! That is like asking a man when did you stop beating your wife. It is hardly a fair question.

HUME-WILLIAMS holds up a second paper.

HUME-WILLIAMS Here now is an article, which you wrote, protesting negative critiques of the play, *Salome*.
LORD ALFRED DOUGLAS Yes yes, another familiar staple of this Court, which I wrote as an undergraduate student in 1895.
BILLING When he was trapped by Oscar Wilde!
HUME-WILLIAMS You wrote, Lord Alfred Douglas: "I suppose *Salome* is indeed unhealthy, unwholesome and un-English, for there is no representation in it of quiet domestic life, nobody slaps anyone else on the back, and there is not a single reference to roast beef. But the less aggressively mundane will find in Mr. Wilde's tragedy the beauty of a perfect work of art, and honey of sweet bitter thoughts."
LORD ALFRED DOUGLAS There you are.
HUME-WILLIAMS This is your opinion of the play?
LORD ALFRED DOUGLAS It is exactly the same opinion as your supposed client, Maud Allan. The difference is that I escaped from its influence, while she remains under it. I was naively defending Wilde then as you are now.
HUME-WILLIAMS You defended Wilde.
LORD ALFRED DOUGLAS Then! Not now!
HUME-WILLIAMS Allow me to put to you one last letter, written by your own hand, if I am not mistaken. Is this indeed your handwriting?
LORD ALFRED DOUGLAS If you show me a letter in my handwriting

I give you fair warning that I shall tear it up. It is a stolen letter, stolen by a blackmailer! And you having it there makes you a partner in that crime!

JUDGE DARLING Hold it up to him, but out of his reach.

LORD ALFRED DOUGLAS *(waves it away)* Yes it is my handwriting!

HUME-WILLIAMS This is a letter written by you on 9 June, 1895, to the editor of *Truth*, who had attacked you in that publication for leaving Wilde in the lurch by not testifying on his behalf during his trial, and who further wrote that the acts for which Wilde was condemned were in fact not practiced by others, to which you replied: "I personally know forty or fifty men who practice these acts. Men in the best society, members of Parliament even. In a few days I will send to you and to every judge, lawyer and legislator in England, a special plea written to advocate what I maintain, that these tastes are perfectly natural, biological tendencies in certain people and that the law has no right to interfere with them. Mr. Wilde's case was said to be one of moral outrage, but as you must know, in France, Italy, and Germany as well, such discriminatory laws have been either abolished or modified. Our country alone has refused to take any cognizance of the known and admitted facts of modern medical science. ...I confess I have not many hopes for the present age. But ultimate liberation from the slavery of conventional prejudice is as inevitable as death." ...Lord Alfred Douglas, that period you hoped for in which sodomy, unchecked by law, will flourish, has not yet arrived?

LORD ALFRED DOUGLAS On the contrary, I do think it has. At the time I wrote that letter, sodomy was condemned by all decent people.

HUME-WILLIAMS You were not a decent person?

LORD ALFRED DOUGLAS No I was not, and I have said so. Much good may it do you.

HUME-WILLIAMS Thank you, Lord Alfred Douglas.

LORD ALFRED DOUGLAS somewhat folds in on himself, exhausted.

BILLING My Lord, may I cross-examine the witness?

JUDGE DARLING If you must.

BILLING Lord Alfred Douglas, certain letters have been read to you.

LORD ALFRED DOUGLAS Indeed.

BILLING You wrote in one letter that the best men in the best society, including members of Parliament, were all sodomites?

LORD ALFRED DOUGLAS That is a fact, now more so than ever.

BILLING And what has been done about the matter?

LORD ALFRED DOUGLAS I have written letters. I have gone to Scotland Yard to complain about male prostitutes being allowed to ply their trade in Piccadilly. But they told me they were not permitted to do anything, that their hands were tied.

BILLING Do you consider this a political matter?

LORD ALFRED DOUGLAS Yes.

BILLING For which people can be subjected to blackmail?

LORD ALFRED DOUGLAS looks up at BILLING.

LORD ALFRED DOUGLAS ...I have been blackmailed all my life. I am blackmailed still. I was blackmailed to prevent me coming to this Court, told that if I come I will be abused, held up to scorn, to ridicule and contempt. And so it has been done. The past, about which one can do nothing but repent and do ones best to carry on with dignity, has been hurled in my face time and again by lawyers and politicians entirely for their own benefit and at my expense. As far as I can tell, this world they claim to serve with their persecutions has not improved one bit as a result. Better to live like dogs in No Man's Land than in such a world.

BILLING And yet in spite of that, in the public interest, you come here to tell this Court the truth?

LORD ALFRED DOUGLAS *(wrecked inside by the irony of his answer:)* ...Yes.

BILLING Thank you, Lord Alfred Douglas. That is all.

Music – Grieg's "Peer Gynt Suit No.1, Op.46: 2. Aasa's Death." DOUGLAS steps down and makes his exit, exchanging a mutual look with MAUD that holds years of unhappiness.

Scene Twelve

Music continues a bit into JUDGE DARLING's opening remarks.

JUDGE DARLING Gentlemen of the jury.

TITLE: "3 June, 1918. Day Five, the final day of the trial."

JUDGE DARLING You have heard the evidence and arguments on both sides. The actual subject of the drama therein has been and remains the paragraph titled "The Cult of the Clitoris," published by the defendant, Noel Pemberton-Billing, in his paper, *The Vigilante*. The question for the Jury to decide is whether that paragraph constitutes a libel upon Miss Allan, whether its claims have been proven true, and whether it was indeed published for the public benefit. And as to all this about the Forty-seven Thousand and German agents and whose name may or may not be listed in some Black Book somewhere, I shall rule that these matters are absolutely irrelevant to this case, and that the Jury shall not consider them.

BILLING Am I to understand, that in my final address, I am not allowed to make any reference to the evidence brought forward in connection with the

Black Book?

JUDGE DARLING I have said what I have said, –

BILLING / –My Lord–!

JUDGE DARLING –and I hope you understand: it is absolutely immaterial for you to address the Jury with regard to anything other than that paragraph. Now, your audience awaits you, Mr. Billing, should you care to speak to them.

BILLING ...Ladies and gentlemen. And gentlemen of the Jury. There must be a reason why our nation's position in this war is worse today than it was when it started. The best blood of this country is already spilled; and do you think that I am going to keep quiet in my position as a public man while nine men die every minute for our mistakes? I want to know why those mistakes have occurred, and to bring our nation out of this war a little cleaner than it was when it went in. That is my crime. And I plead guilty to it.

I was so convinced of the gravity of this situation that for the last two and a half years I have been libelling public men – knowingly libelling them – in the pages of my newspaper. Surely, I thought, they would call me to task and in a public Court expose the reasons for all the regrettable incidents of this war. But not one man came forward. Why?

Ladies and Gentlemen, the witnesses I have presented to you came here to speak the truth. I believed what these witnesses had to say. Their testimony made sense of the many mistakes, tragedies, and regrettable affairs of this war, not to mention the apathy and protection which our enemies, still allowed to live in this country, and their sympathizers, continue to receive despite the average citizen's struggle to get a square job or a square deal.

In the evidence I have brought before you we have caught a glimpse of that mysterious influence which is sterilizing our nation. Such a play as Oscar Wilde's *Salome*, calculated to do terrible harm to all who see it by undermining their moral strength of will, such a play does more damage in the end than the German army itself. And as for the supposed centerpiece of this alleged libel, I had never heard the word "clitoris" in my life before Captain Spencer brought it to my attention. I asked him what it referred to, and he explained to me what had been verified to him by medical authority, that it is the idol of a cult dedicated to all forms of sexual perversion, a cult with a common language, a common secret, a common guilt.

Can decent people stand by and allow such monsters to be aroused against the public interest in a time of national emergency? No we cannot. I have not stood by. I have done my duty. I ask now that the gentlemen of the jury do theirs, and send me away from this place with the confidence a verdict of my countrymen will give me to carry on the heavy task which, in the interests of my country, I have seen fit to undertake. Thank you.

Enthusiastic applause from some. JUDGE DARLING attempts to quiet it with his gavel. From now until the end of the trial, MAUD is in tears.

JUDGE DARLING Mr. Hume-Williams.

HUME-WILLIAMS Gentlemen of the Jury. It is one of the curious, most regrettable incidents of this war, that the imagination of people seems to be inflamed to such a point that almost anything is believable. Now we listen with rapt attention to things we would have laughed away as ridiculous before the war. But today: every tale, every yarn, however silly, obtains some credence.

It is not an easy task to represent Miss Maud Allan under these circumstances, and the belligerent manner in which the defendant, Mr. Pemberton-Billing, has thought fit to conduct this case. If the two-and-a-half years of libelling he just now admitted to you having done were met with no response, it is, of course, because he never once mentioned an individual name. Having finally realized this, Mr. Billing chose not one among the high ranking men he claims to be protecting this country against, but rather a dancer, who has nothing to do with the politics of this nation. Mr. Billing had realized what he must do. Nobody was listening to him; and so he needed something gaudy to attract the mob's attention, curry their favor, and bring out his fairy tale of German princes, secret books and salacious perversions.

"The Cult of the Clitoris!" Was there ever anything more deliberately spectacular? "I stand here before you," says this man, "an apostle of purity, in the interests of public decency." Public decency! To attack a woman! And when she takes the only steps available to her to clear her name, he tells the Jury she is filthy, abandoned, and perverse. He drags out from the past her family misfortunes as evidence, not hesitating to suggest this unfortunate fact proves some sadistic tendency might run in the woman's blood. A lady comes to clear her name, and it is further bloodied under the rake of this man, desperate as he is to sell to you his hysterical propaganda.

Mr. Pemberton-Billing says that everything he claims to be true is so. Has he proved it? From the beginning of this case to the end, no, he has not. ...To you, gentlemen, I entrust not only this woman's reputation, but the sanity and good sense of our nation. Thank you.

JUDGE DARLING Ladies and gentleman, you will be glad to know that I really do not think there is anything more to be said on this matter. It is now for the gentlemen of the Jury to decide. Please retire to consider the relevant evidence and determine your verdict.

JUDGE DARLING hits his gavel. SOLDIERS ONE THROUGH SIX all return to their places in the trench and stand there, leaving MAUD standing alone and separately. Once ALL are in place, SOLDIER SIX pulls out his pocket watch and looks at it. The sound of its ticking can be heard. The OTHERS regard him soberly. THEY affix their bayonets to the ends of their rifles, then sit, guns ready, helmets on, and pull out their carefully wrapped, partially eaten chocolate bars. Each of them breaks off one square and eats it. SOLDIER SIX continues to keep his eye on his watch.

Scene Thirteen

SOLDIER THREE stands and becomes OSCAR WILDE. MAUD watches OSCAR WILDE, now haggard, as he wearily takes a seat at a cafe table in Paris. Music – "Ave Maria. Ellen's Gesang III, D.839." The ticking of the watch fades. OSCAR WILDE pours himself a glass of wine. He savors a sip from it. He notices MAUD.

OSCAR WILDE ...Do you know me?

MAUD ALLAN No...?

OSCAR WILDE How unfortunate. I was hoping someone who knows me might pass by and take pity. You see I haven't any money to pay for this wine. I shall have to keep ordering more until someone comes. It's a little game I often lose. ...Won't *you* join me?

MAUD does. OSCAR fills his glass a bit more and offers it to MAUD. She takes a sip, then sets it down again.

MAUD ALLAN Thank you... I do remember now. Oscar Wilde. We did meet once.

OSCAR WILDE Did we after all? I should think I would recall meeting a woman with such sumptuous taste in dresses. When was it?

MAUD ALLAN It was in Paris. It must have been shortly before y– ...Well.

OSCAR WILDE Ah, yes. Well. And what did we talk about?

MAUD ALLAN An accident, as I recall it.

OSCAR WILDE ...Yes! Yes, I had that day seen a woman throw herself into the Seine, and was still quite anxious over it. A sailor eventually rescued her. ...I could have rescued her. But this act was forbidden me. I would have seemed to be seeking attention for myself and it would have made a scandal. Yes. It's horrible. But after my trial, heroism and good deeds were forbidden me... What else did we discuss?

MAUD ALLAN You remarked on my American accent. And we talked about language.

OSCAR WILDE Oh, I'm sure. Have you noticed at all how language has declined over the years, since being denied my genius with it?

MAUD ALLAN Has it?

OSCAR WILDE Oh yes, it has become so sterile, so intolerably dull and unromantic. It's a wonder we can understand anything at all. Take this war business that's all the rage just now. Warriors are now merely soldiers.

A glorious battle is an action, perhaps an incursion, sometimes even an engagement, as if it were but a social appointment between two estranged acquaintances. And the sweet red wine of youth is now blood at best and at worst a vital fluid. These military and other official people now always disguise the horribleness of their actions with benumbed words. They dare not name the things of which they speak. Words without feeling make no sense. Occasionally one is still allowed to be thrust into battle to penetrate the enemy, in which case a glimmer of passion can yet be perceived, and war is at least granted the innuendo of the sexual perversion one always suspected it to be.

MAUD ALLAN I've had my fill of innuendo.

OSCAR WILDE And of war?

MAUD ALLAN I have had nothing to do with that! All I have ever wished was to make my art. And to forget. Nobody will let me do either.

OSCAR WILDE Regardless of anybody, your two wishes are hardly compatible if I may say it. Art is memory. As for war, I have begun to think it may very well constitute the permanent condition of mankind. When the enlightened men finally bring down the curtain on this war, and they will, the lights will rise on the good British people and they'll feel themselves emerge from the dark, not realizing it's merely intermission. During the interval, they'll check their wallets. Those who can manage it will sip some champagne and have a laugh about Lady So-and-so's décolletage. Those who find themselves of a serious disposition might even attempt a critique of the little drama that's passed. Then, soon enough, the lights will dim again; and back into the theater of war they will march. For mankind is not yet so fabulous as to rise above brutality and linger on the beauty of this world. ...How sad for mankind. ...Still, there is some relief. Art will win this war in the end, when memory reaches not for cold statistics, but for exquisite music, brilliant novels and eloquent poems, that it may touch the true feelings of this time.

MAUD ALLAN *(determined)* Nobody knows my feelings. And no one ever shall.

OSCAR WILDE ...Tell me, if he is found Not Guilty, what will you do?

MAUD ALLAN *(lost)* ...I don't know.

OSCAR WILDE If I may offer you one bit of advice, learned from hard experience. Always forgive your enemies. Nothing annoys them so much.

> *MAUD laughs. This pleases OSCAR, who looks at her for a moment.*

OSCAR WILDE ...Thank you, my dear.

MAUD ALLAN What for?

OSCAR WILDE For remembering our having met. ...And for dressing so divinely for our reunion. ...May I ask one more favor.

MAUD ALLAN What is it?

OSCAR WILDE Remember that I could have rescued that woman.
MAUD ALLAN ...I will.

> *OSCAR WILDE takes one last drink. He stands, then pulls out from his coat a newspaper, which he regards solemnly. OSCAR WILDE walks back toward the trench, tossing the paper down on the ground along the way.*

Scene Fourteen

> *Shift.*

SOLDIER ONE This just in, men!

> *SOLDIERS TWO, FOUR and FIVE all respond with general appreciation.*

SOLDIER SIX It'll have to wait. We don't have time now, lads.
SOLDIER TWO But the verdict.

> *SOLDIER ONE stands and goes for the newspaper.*

SOLDIER SIX Sit down. It can wait.
SOLDIER FOUR Bugger off! Read it.
SOLDIER FIVE What's the headline?
SOLDIER TWO Yes, what's the verdict?
SOLDIER SIX Be ready, lads!
SOLDIER ONE Noel Pemberton-Billing,
SOLDIER SIX Here
SOLDIER ONE is
SOLDIER SIX we
SOLDIER ONE Not Guilty!

> *Huge applause explodes in the air.*

SOLDIER SIX Go!

> *A bomb drops and machine gunfire rips through the air.*

SOLDIER SIX Go! Go!

> *THE SOLDIERS all rush over the top, some still distracted by their excitement over the verdict, and ALL are immediately gunned down. Red poppy petals explode where blood should spurt and spatter.*

The SOLDIERS all appear dead. MAUD remains standing. The applause continues, now more distant. The shelling and gunfire is now also quite distant. MAUD makes her way slowly from soldier to soldier, checking the face of each. The applause dies away when she gets near SOLDIER SIX:

SOLDIER SIX Sara. Sara.

SOLDIER SIX dies. The distant shelling and gunfire also dies away, leaving only Mathilde and a wind sweeping gently across No Man's Land.

SOLDIER ONE Maud? Maudie?

MAUD rushes to SOLDIER ONE and turns him over.

MAUD ALLAN Shhh...

MAUD kisses SOLDIER ONE delicately on the mouth. SOLDIER ONE dies. MAUD speaks to him, holding his hand and rubbing his hair.

MAUD ALLAN There was a bitter taste on thy lips. Was it the taste of blood? Nay. But perchance it was the taste of love. They say that love hath a bitter taste. But what matter? What matter?

MAUD is alone. Mathilde sings in the setting sun.

The end.

Notes on the Plays

God's Plot

I first heard of *Ye Bare and Ye Cubb*—written in 1665, and the first known play to be produced in the future USA—at a 1997 lecture given by theater director Anne Bogart. No copy of the script has survived the centuries. And from what little documentation she found on it, Bogart concluded that the supposed satire and its legal battle was an early example of the American habit of separating art from politics, which would eventually reach a dramatic high (or rather low) point during the McCarthy era.

More recently, Joel Eis wrote a thoroughly researched book collecting every scrap of evidence he could find on the case, suggesting that the incident was not only about art and politics, but also religious conflict, economics, land fraud, false identity, entrepreneurialism, community, the spirit of independence, and a host of other issues near and dear to the American heart. It seemed this little-known blip on the timeline of our nation's history actually contained nearly all the seeds of our national character.

Given the political nature of the subject, during the process of the original production I was asked on several occasions what the play's intended message was. The question always struck me because in writing *God's Plot* I didn't consciously set out to deliver a message. The historical incident itself encompasses so many potent themes and ideas, all debatable, and I tried to allow them to remain as such. I simply wanted to tell this great story that got under my skin, moved me, excited me, made me laugh, reminded me of my failings, and encouraged me to continue to "go west." By that I mean to explore the open range of my thinking, my actions, and the choices I might make in relation to the many people who are all my neighbors. This story and its distant figures remind me of who I am as an American—with all my pluses and minuses vying for dominance in one messy body.

I would say, though, that the play does consciously ask at least one specific, basic question about the warring sides of our national character. A verse that was cut from Tryal Pore's final anthem during rehearsals for the original production, and which remains central for me nonetheless, poses this question well, I think:

> One side damns, the other longs.
> But a good face separates our rights from wrongs.
> And I hope we never act in only throngs.
> Can we stay one yet be many?

Mary Stuart

I had not yet seen an English-language production of *Maria Stuart* at the time I adapted it, though Schiller's play has been done in English innumerable times. The first German production that I saw was performed, oddly, in a kind of pseudo Mexican street theater style, with touches of commedia and Balinese theater thrown in, and a single male actor portraying both queens. It was a peculiar introduction to Schiller's play.

Nevertheless, I still remember the image of one actor playing both queens, which effectively, if perhaps too obviously, highlighted their innate connection. To express their difference, the actor carried a small leather purse, on one side of which a burning heart was embroidered in rubies (Mary) and on the other a crown in gold (Elizabeth). The conflict between the heart and head did not only exist between two people, but within the individual. It was this conflict that struck my initial interest in Schiller's play.

When I finally read the play in English, though Schiller's exquisitely structured plot got my heart racing, the fidelity with which the various English and Scottish translators whose versions I read maintained the original's Romantic-era excesses seemed to slow down what impressed me as a remarkably contemporary dramatic situation, a fast-moving, juicy political thriller that could easily take place today in the UK, Germany, or America. So I decided to take a crack at adapting the play myself. Though I ended up cutting quite a lot, I found that indeed nothing needed to be added to make the play "relevant to today." It already is.

Like Shakespeare, Schiller was not at all concerned with either historical idealism or accuracy, but rather used his source material as the spark to fan a blazing drama. In this regard, the German playwright's dramatic take on the historical British Queen Elizabeth is a particularly refreshing example. Gone is the BBC-reverence for the great icon. In Schiller's hands she is a deeply complicated human being.

I love the messy psychology Schiller granted all his characters, how they contradict themselves and do battle with their moral conundrums. I'm also fascinated by the collision of times, places and cultures to be found in a contemporary American production of a two-hundred-year-old German play based on four-hundred-year-old British history. Schiller captured something internationally and eternally human when, through *Maria Stuart*, he posed an important question that it seems every generation of every culture must answer. What do we do when our system of justice, our sense of morality, and our own personal desires don't meet eye to eye?

Salomania

In 2006 I directed Oscar Wilde's *Salome* for the Aurora Theatre Company, my first gig there. In a book on the play's production history, I came across a handful of pages summarizing the striking 1918 libel case of Maud Allan v. Noel Pemberton-Billing. Intrigued, I tracked down two books that had been written about the trial itself, as well as a biography of Maud Allan and another of her brother, Theodore Durrant. I also read up on the British perspective of WWI, and the literature and other art that tried to articulate that unprecedented war. When Tom Ross, the artistic director at Aurora, approached me in 2009 about commissioning a new play, *Salomania* was my immediate suggestion.

Cracking the nut of how to structure a play about this unwieldy bit of history proved difficult at first. The plot roams from San Francisco to Germany before settling in London, and involves an extensive cast of anonymous nobodies and prominent somebodies, among them a defiantly enigmatic central figure in Maud Allan. Without writing a six-hour play requiring a couple dozen actors, how could I capture this sprawling, epic event in all its complicated, intriguing absurdity? Then Tom made the suggestion that I take the cast list of Wilde's *Salome* and apply it to my own. Maud Allan would be Salome. Pemberton-Billing would be John the Baptist. Judge Darling would be Herod. I didn't end up doing that. But from Tom's suggestion came the idea to cast a troupe of soldiers in all the other roles. This not only allowed me to justify a small cast of seven actors playing multiple parts—a casting practice I don't like to do without an organic artistic justification—but, more importantly, it provided a means of capturing the surreal juxtaposition of life in the trench with life on the home front. In that regard, that a dancer was at the center of the play's subject also helped. Dance and dance-theater make their impact by juxtaposing actions, images, and sounds with implicit rather than explicit meanings, allowing a gap for the audience to fill with their imaginations. The play's dramaturgy followed suit, butting contrasting locations, events, time periods, and aesthetics up against one another. Stark and strange juxtapositions, a trademark of WWI, extended into Nina Ball's set design, which in one space contained all the places visited by the play; and Callie Floor's costume design, by which dirty soldier pants and boots could often be seen beneath glitzy society gowns or well-pressed British law regalia.

Salomania depicts the actions and counter-actions taken by a range of individuals at a crucial and decisive moment in our world's history, when new technology yielded unprecedented horror in the trenches and those back home faced a disorienting onslaught of social and moral change. With its fractured approach, the play expresses the messy human experience of anxiety in a time of incredible flux. Ultimately, *Salomania* is less about its individual characters than it is about the hysterical society that shaped them. What those involved in these particular events felt inside, and much with regard to their true motives, remains a mystery about which one is free to speculate, as many historians interested in this trial and its era have done and continue to do. In writing *Salomania* I was careful not to be so presumptuous as to clarify that mystery. What then would be the point of the play? It was in fact the baffling question as to how so many intelligent, prominent people could say and do so many stunningly outrageous things that grabbed a lasting hold of me when I first encountered this story. How can a society allow itself to be both hysterical and "civilized" at the same time, and expect to function either well, morally, or respectably? Not having an answer to that question has continued to compel me. It's my hope that the play does the same for most who encounter it.

Considering all that, it is appropriate that *Salomania* be a demanding play. It demands a lot from its actors, designers, and crew. It likewise demands something of its audience. In my personal estimation, *Salomania* holds a special position in this volume. I consider it the most mature work overall that I have written to date. Of course that's me saying that, and I understand there are funny ideas out there about objectivity and who gets to say what about an artist's work. Anyway, if I manage again to write something near to this play's particular combination of theatricality, language, density of theme, specificity of character, truthfulness in expressing a given moment in time, and pertinence to the present moment, I'll be very glad. That it came together in this instance as it did might ultimately be due to the fact that my respect for the subject compelled me to do my best to do right by it.

Finally, in addition to asking questions, if *Salomania* does also say something it might be that truth, beauty, and sanity are important, and not at all unrelated. This is but one of the vital lessons I took from these nearly 100-year-old, disturbingly contemporary events.

About the Author

Mark Jackson is a playwright, director and performer. He was Artistic Director of Art Street Theatre, San Francisco, from 1995 to 2004, during which time he wrote, directed, and performed in numerous productions for the company. Mark's work has also been seen at Aurora Theatre Company, Encore Theatre Company, EXIT Theatre, Potrzebie Dance Project, San Francisco International Arts Festival, The Shotgun Players, Z Space, The Catamounts (Denver), and The Studio Theatre (Washington D.C.), among others; as well as internationally at Arts International Festival IV (Japan), Edinburgh Festival Fringe (UK), and Deutsches Theater Berlin (Germany). His plays have been developed at American Conservatory Theater, Capital Stage, EXIT Theatre, Magic Theatre, Playwrights Foundation, and Z Space. EXIT Press published *TEN PLAYS*, the first collection of Mark's work, in 2010.

Mark has been a resident playwright of the Djerassi Resident Artists Program, where he was awarded the William and Flora Hewlett Foundation Honorary Fellowship. He is a German Chancellor Fellow of the Alexander von Humboldt Foundation, which took him to Berlin, Germany, to work with Mime Centrum Berlin, a practical research center for physical theatre. Some other awards and honors include the Edgerton Foundation New American Plays Award, a Magic Theatre / Z Space New Works Initiative commission, and the *San Francisco Bay Guardian* Goldie Award. Mark's writing has benefited numerous times from the generosity of the Tournesol Project, a granting program for the development of new work. He has been a company member of The Shotgun Players since 2010.

Mark is a graduate of the San Francisco State University Theatre Arts Department. He lives in San Francisco with his talented and beautiful actor/singer gal pal, Beth Wilmurt. Their apartment is rent-controlled, so there they stay.

More Plays From EXIT Press

Ten Plays by Mark Jackson
"From reimagined Shakespearean classics (*R&J, I Am Hamlet*) to Jackson's breakout hit *The Death of Meyerhold*, the bleakly comedic *American $uicide*, and the stirring Kurosawa-esque epic *The Forest War*, what these plays have in common is an audacious commitment to the illimitable possibilities of live theater" — Nicole Gluckstern, SF Bay Guardian

Woyzeck, Pelleas and Melisande, Ubu Roi: translated by Rob Melrose
"Rob Melrose is a kind of magician, and his theater, Cutting Ball, is one of the most exciting and integrity-filled enterprises going in the sometimes-shabby field of the American theater. These translations, lucid and sharp, are a beautiful testimony to the value of Rob's achievement." — Oskar Eustis

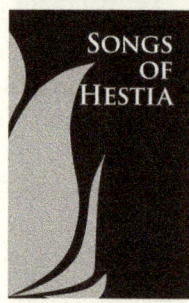

Songs of Hestia: Plays From the 2010 San Francisco Olympians Festival
Playwrights Nirmala Nataraj, Bennett Fisher, Stuart Eugene Bousel, Claire Rice, and Evelyn Jean Pine adapt some of Western culture's oldest stories, illuminating our present-day concerns with imagination, creativity, curiosity and passion.

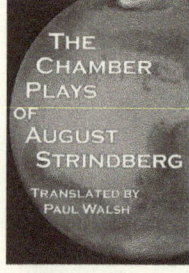

The Chamber Plays of August Strindberg
New translations by Yale Professor Paul Walsh of Strindberg's five intimate chamber plays: *Storm*, *Burned House*, *The Ghost Sonata*, *The Pelican*, and *The Black Glove*.

EXIT Press is the publishing division of EXIT Theatre, a San Francisco theater company that was founded in 1983. Coming soon are *Plays from the 2011 San Francisco Olympians Festival* and books of plays by Elisa de Carlo, Sarah McKereghan and Sean Owens.
www.exitpress.org

www.ingramcontent.com/pod-product-compliance
Lightning Source LLC
Chambersburg PA
CBHW032116090426
42743CB00007B/370